Pocket
LISBON
TOP SIGHTS • LOCAL LIFE • MADE EASY

Kerry Christiani

In This Book

QuickStart Guide

Your keys to understanding the city – we help you decide what to do and how to do it

Need to Know
Tips for a smooth trip

Neighbourhoods
What's where

Explore Lisbon

The best things to see and do, neighbourhood by neighbourhood

Top Sights
Make the most of your visit

Local Life
The insider's city

The Best of Lisbon

The city's highlights in handy lists to help you plan

Best Walks
See the city on foot

Lisbon's Best...
The best experiences

Survival Guide

Tips and tricks for a seamless, hassle-free city experience

Getting Around
Travel like a local

Essential Information
Including where to stay

Our selection of the city's best places to eat, drink and experience:

◉ **Sights**

✖ **Eating**

🍷 **Drinking**

✦ **Entertainment**

🔒 **Shopping**

These symbols give you the vital information for each listing:

☎ Telephone Numbers	👪 Family-Friendly
◷ Opening Hours	🐾 Pet-Friendly
P Parking	🚌 Bus
⊘ Nonsmoking	🚢 Ferry
@ Internet Access	Ⓜ Metro
🛜 Wi-Fi Access	🚊 Tram
🥗 Vegetarian Selection	🚆 Train
📖 English-Language Menu	

Find each listing quickly on maps for each neighbourhood:

Bar Hemingway

16 🍷 Map p233, B2

Legend has it that Hemi self, wielding a machine rate this timber-pan ered bar during showpiece is a en by Papa ar town. Dress .com; Hôtel Rit ⊙6.30pm-2a

Lonely Planet's Lisbon

Lonely Planet Pocket Guides are designed to get you straight to the heart of the city.

Inside you'll find all the must-see sights, plus tips to make your visit to each one really memorable. We've split the city into easy-to-navigate neighbourhoods and provided clear maps so you'll find your way around with ease. Our expert authors have searched out the best of the city: walks, food, nightlife and shopping, to name a few. Because you want to explore, our 'Local Life' pages will take you to some of the most exciting areas to experience the real Lisbon.

And of course you'll find all the practical tips you need for a smooth trip: itineraries for short visits, how to get around, and how much to tip the guy who serves you a drink at the end of a long day's exploration.

It's your guarantee of a really great experience.

Our Promise

You can trust our travel infor- mation because Lonely Planet authors visit the places we write about, each and every edition. We never accept freebies for positive coverage, so you can rely on us to tell it like it is.

QuickStart Guide 7

Explore Lisbon 21

Worth a Trip:

The Best of Lisbon   125

Lisbon's Best Walks

Lisbon's Best ...

Survival Guide   145

QuickStart Guide

Welcome to Lisbon

A roller-coaster city of seven hills, crowned by a Moorish castle and washed in an artist's pure light, Lisbon is cinematically beautiful and historically compelling. This is a capital city of big skies and bigger vistas; of rumbling trams and Willy Wonka–like elevators; of melancholic fado song and live-to-party nightlife. Edge, charisma and postcard good looks – Lisbon has the lot.

Largo das Portas do Sol (p63)
MANFRED GOTTSCHALK/GETTY IMAGES ©

Lisbon
Top Sights

Mosteiro dos Jerónimos (p78)

A love letter to the Age of Discovery and the nadir of Manueline style, Belém's Unesco-listed monastery is upliftingly beautiful and intricate.

CALLE MONTES/GETTY IMAGES ©

Tram 28 (p56)

You haven't been to Lisbon until you've scooted through the streets on this golden oldie, glimpsing the river, Sé (cathedral) and the pearly dome of Basílica da Estrela as you go.

CHIARA SALVADORI/GETTY IMAGES ©

Castelo de São Jorge (p60) ✦

There are castles and then there are *castles,* and no one knew this better than the Moors, who built this fortress high and mighty. Enjoy wide-angle city and river views from the ramparts.

Oceanário (p90)

Think if you've seen one aquarium, you've seen them all? Don't bank on it. Sharks, penguins on ice and somersaulting sea otters are just the tip of the marine-life iceberg at the humongous Oceanário.

Praça do Comércio ✗ (p42)

Arguably the heart of the Portuguese capital, this square, with its river views, palatial colonnaded buildings, triumphal arch and bee-yellow trams, is the Lisbon you've been dreaming about.

Museu Calouste Gulbenkian (p100)

Vast and fascinating, this is an arts collection you can dip into time and again. Treasures reach from Dutch Master paintings to Egyptian reliefs, Monet originals to René Lalique jewellery.

Convento do Carmo (p24)

Neither time nor the ravages of natural disaster have been able to wipe away the spirit of this Gothic convent, founded for the Carmelite Order in 1389 and reduced to enigmatic ruins in the 1755 earthquake.

Museu Nacional de Arte Antiga (p112)

Lisbon's most remarkable ancient art collection takes shelter in a 17th-century palace. Albrecht Dürer's *St Jerome,* Nuno Gonçalves' magnum opus *Panels of St Vincent* and the gold monstrance of Belém are the stars of the show.

Museu Colecção Berardo (p80)

What do you do if you're a billionaire art collector? If you're José Berardo, you build one of Lisbon's foremost contemporary galleries, fill it with Warhol, Man Ray, Picasso and Miró masterpieces and, as a nice gesture, make it free to visit.

Museu Nacional do Azulejo (p74)

Housed in a meticulously restored Manueline convent, this out-of-the-way museum is an ode to the *azulejo* (tile), with its peerless collection of geometric Hispano-Moorish tiles, Renaissance hunting scenes and a standout baroque panel of pre-1755 Lisbon.

Palácio Nacional de Sintra (p122)

Sintra's Unesco World Heritage palace is pure fairy-tale stuff. Moorish, Manueline and Italian Renaissance styles mingle in halls flamboyantly adorned with *azulejos* (some of Portugal's oldest), frescoes and intricately carved woodwork.

Lisbon Local Life

Insider tips to help you find the real city

True, the castle is grand, but there's more to Lisbon than a handful of icons. Once you've visited the show-stoppers, it's time to explore labyrinthine Moorish alleyways, arty enclaves, old-fashioned stores and one-of-a-kind bars: the Lisbon locals know and love.

Strolling Príncipe Real (p38)

▶ Art & design
▶ People-watching cafes

Easygoing Príncipe Real provides a satisfying slice of daily life in leafy squares, avant-garde design shops, fashion boutiques and retro-cool cafes. Sights are few, but this area is full of creative verve and bohemian flair, making it perfect for a lazy brunch or afternoon mooch.

Alfama Backstreets (p62)

▶ Magical views
▶ Hidden laneways

Delve into the disorientating alleys of Moorish Alfama and who knows what you might find? Chefs firing up their barbecues, kids playing in front of sun-bleached chapels, impromptu fado gigs. Alfama – and neighbouring Castelo and Graça – will leave you smitten with their hidden nooks, castle-facing *miradouros* (viewpoints) and tangible sense of history.

Baixa Back in Time (p44)

▶ Old-world shops
▶ Backstreets

Slip back to an age where purchases were still hand-wrapped, shop owners knew customers by name and stores traded solely in tinned fish, buttons and bowler hats in the winding laneways of Baixa and Rossio. At dusk, toast the past Lisbon-style with *ginjinha* (cherry liqueur).

Cais do Sodré Bar Crawl (p26)

▶ Bar-hopping
▶ Postmidnight parties

Tune into Lisbon's hottest nightlife scene in the grim-turned-glam neighbourhood of Cais do Sodré. A makeover has revamped the formerly red-light Rua Nova do Carvalho, whose bordello-chic bars and burlesque clubs are now *the* place to be after midnight.

Street dining in Cais do Sodré (p26)

Alfama (p62)

Other great places and ways to experience the city like a local:

LX Factory (p117)

Biking the Tejo (p30)

Shop 'n' Stroll (p36)

Mercado da Ribeira (p37)

Coffee Culture (p33)

Cristo Rei (p50)

Exploring the Avenida (p109)

Have Your Cake (p32)

Ginjinha (p52)

Lisbon Day Planner

Day One

This one-day itinerary focuses on the city's show-stoppers. Begin at the heart of the city, **Praça do Comércio** (p42), strolling past its regal colonnaded buildings and triumphal arch to the riverfront. Then follow the tram tracks up to Gothic **Sé** (cathedral; p66) and the bougainvillea-draped **Miradouro de Santa Luzia** (p62) for spirit-soaring views.

Sip a drink and peer across Alfama's jigsaw of rooftops at **Largo das Portas do Sol** (p63). From here, cobbled lanes twist quaintly up to the ramparts of Moorish **Castelo de São Jorge** (p60), where you can romp through millennia of local history. Spend the rest of the afternoon moseying around old-world stores in **Baixa** (p44), picking up treats from retro-tinned fish to vintage garb and port. For a 360-degree panorama, ride the neo-Gothic **Elevador de Santa Justa** (p47).

Back down at street level, head to **Rossio** (p47) and cross over to cupboard-sized **A Ginjinha** (p52) for a shot of cherry liqueur with the locals. An evening meander through Alfama's mazy, lantern-lit lanes works up an appetite for a courtyard dinner at **Santo António de Alfama** (p68) or a fado-filled night at convivial **A Baîuca** (p70).

Day Two

Board vintage **tram 28** (p56) at Praça Martim Moniz for an early-morning spin through Lisbon's hilly streets, with fleeting views of the river and trophy sights. Get off to explore the lavish interior of neoclassical **Basílica da Estrela** (p116) and palm-fringed **Jardim da Estrela** (p116) opposite. The **Palácio da Assembleia da República** (p116), Portugal's parliament, stands nearby.

Take the same tram back to Chiado, stopping for coffee and people-watching on the terrace of art-nouveau **Café a Brasileira** (p57). Linger in Chiado, where speciality shops and boutiques purvey everything from handmade gloves to designer fashion. You can imagine the full thrust of the 1755 earthquake surveying the ruins at **Convento do Carmo** (p24), atmospherically perched above the city.

From Chiado, amble along Rua do Loreto, then down to **Miradouro de Santa Catarina** (p31) for sundowners and twinkling city views at **Noobai Café** (p34). **Pharmacia** (p32), just steps away, is an original choice for dinner. Glide downhill on the nearby **Elevador da Bica** (p31) and wander slightly east to **Cais do Sodré** (p26) for a late-night bar crawl in Lisbon's most happening nightlife district.

Short on time?
We've arranged Lisbon's must-sees into these day-by-day itineraries to make sure you see the very best of the city in the time you have available.

Day Three

☀ Day three begins sweetly over oven-warm *pastéis de nata* (custard tarts) in the tiled rooms of **Antiga Confeitaria de Belém** (p85). Then it's over to the Unesco World Heritage-listed **Mosteiro dos Jerónimos** (p78) for a gargoyle's-eye view of its exuberant Manueline church and cloister before the crowds arrive. Cut through the box-hedge-fringed gardens opposite to reach the **Padrão dos Descobrimentos** (p83), the ship-shaped monument festooned with Age of Discovery heroes.

☀ Lunch at convivial bistro **2 a 8** (p86) stands you in good stead for a brisk walk along the riverfront to the landmark Manueline fortress **Torre de Belém** (p83). Cool off with a drink by the marina before making your way to the contemporary **Museu Colecção Berardo** (p80) for a free feast of Picasso, Warhol, Miró and more.

☾ If you're in the mood for something special, go for the seasonally inspired tasting menu at Michelin-starred **Feitoria** (p86), presuming you've booked ahead. An atmospheric alternative is **Espaço Espelho d'Água** (p86), with cracking river views and a colonial-inspired menu.

Day Four *Sintra*

☀ Ease into day four gently with a saunter along boutique-lined **Avenida da Liberdade** (p109). After a light, healthy lunch at **Os Tibetanos** (p105) or **Cinemateca Portuguesa** (p106), move on to the green heights of **Parque Eduardo VII** (p104) for sweeping city views. A quick metro ride drops you off near the **Museu Calouste Gulbenkian** (p100), containing masterpieces from Rembrandt paintings to René Lalique's impossibly delicate art-nouveau jewellery.

☀ Back on the metro, go east to architecturally innovative Parque das Nações, built for Expo '98. A riverside stroll takes you through lush colonial-inspired gardens to **Ponte Vasco da Gama** (p93), Europe's longest cable-style bridge at 17.2km. Round out your afternoon at the subaquatic **Oceanário** (p90), contemplating playful sea otters, sharks and a kaleidoscope of fish.

☾ Linger for dinner and dreamy Tejo views at the glass-walled **River Lounge** (p96), or head back into the centre and much-lauded **Assinatura** (p106), playing up contemporary Portuguese cuisine. End your trip on a high at the **Sky Bar** (p108), the Tivoli's fashionable rooftop cocktail bar.

Need to Know

**For more information,
see Survival Guide (p145)**

Currency
Euro (€)

Language
Portuguese

Visas
EU nationals need no visa. US, Canadian, Australian and New Zealand visitors can stay for up to 90 days without a visa.

Money
ATMs widely available. Credit cards generally accepted, but cash preferred in some small shops and restaurants. Ask first.

Mobile Phones
European and Australian mobile phones work. US visitors should check with their service provider. Cut the cost of roaming charges by buying a local SIM card.

Time
Lisbon is on GMT/UTC.

Plugs & Adaptors
Plugs have two round pins; electrical current is 220V. North American, UK, Australian and Canadian visitors will need an adaptor.

Tipping
Tip 5% to 10% if you are satisfied with the service. *Serviço* (service charge) is usually only included in the bill at top-end restaurants.

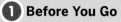

❶ Before You Go

Your Daily Budget

Budget less than €60
▶ Dorm bed €15-25
▶ Make the most of daily specials and fixed-price menus
▶ Plan sightseeing around free admission days (usually Sunday mornings)

Midrange €60–150
▶ Double room in a central hotel €60–120
▶ Meal in a midrange restaurant €20–30
▶ Walking or cycling tour of the city €15–35

Top end more than €150
▶ Boutique hotel room from €120
▶ Three-course dinner with wine from €50
▶ Night at a fado club €50

Useful Websites

Lonely Planet (www.lonelyplanet.com/lisbon) Destination information, hotel bookings, traveller forum and more.

Visit Lisboa (www.visitlisboa.com) Comprehensive tourist office website.

Lisbon Lux (www.lisbonlux.com) City guide.

Spotted by Locals (www.spottedbylocals.com/lisbon) Insider tips.

Advance Planning

One month before Book top-end restaurants, theatre and opera tickets, and excursions. Brush up on your Portuguese.

Two weeks before Buy tickets for gigs and reserve a table in a fado club.

A few days before Check out what's happening on event websites and bone up on your Portuguese wine knowledge on www.viniportugal.pt.

② Arriving in Lisbon

Most international visitors arrive at Lisbon Airport (www.ana.pt), 8km northeast of the city. Bus connections to the centre run frequently. The quickest way to reach the centre is by taking the metro or the AeroBus (www.yellowbustours.com). Buses depart in front of the arrivals hall.

✈ From Lisbon Airport

Destination	Best Transport
Marquês de Pombal & Avenida da Liberdade	AeroBus (line 1), metro
Rossio & Restauradores	AeroBus (line 1), metro
Praça do Comércio	AeroBus (line 1), metro
Cais do Sodré	AeroBus (line 1), metro
Oriente	AeroBus (line 2), metro, bus 708

✈ At the Airport

Lisbon Airport The airport is modern and easy to navigate. In the departures hall you'll find ATMs, baby-changing facilities, a post office and numerous cafes, bars, restaurants and shops. The arrivals hall has ATMs, exchange bureaux, car rental and left luggage, as well as a handy tourist information point where you can pick up brochures and maps.

③ Getting Around

Lisbon's public transport network is cheap and efficient. Save time and money with multiple trips by buying a 24-hour pass (€6), covering buses, trams, funiculars and the metro. For timetables, routes and fares, see www.carris.pt and www.metrolisboa.pt. Much of Bairro Alto, Baixa and Alfama are pedestrian-only – walking is the way to go.

Ⓜ Metro

Lisbon's compact, four-line metro network is particularly handy for reaching the airport, Oriente (Parque das Nações), Marquês de Pombal and São Sebastião (Museu Calouste Gulbenkian, Centro de Arte Moderna). It runs from 6.30am to 1am. Single tickets cost €1.40.

🚊 Tram

For sightseeing on the go, you can't beat Lisbon's trams. Tram 28 is the star route, trundling through Baixa, Alfama, Bairro Alto and Estrela, and affording great views. Other useful routes include tram 15 (for Belém and Alcântara). Single tickets cost €2.85.

🚌 Bus

Lisbon's buses are your best bet for reaching neighbourhoods further out. Useful routes include bus 758 Cais do Sodré to Benfica via Rato and Príncipe Real. Avoid rush hour if you can. Single tickets cost €1.80.

🚕 Taxi

There are taxi ranks at Rossio and Praça dos Restauradores, and near stations and ferry terminals. The flag fall is €2.50 (check the meter). Surcharges apply after 9pm and for carrying luggage.

🚲 Bicycle

The cycling path that shadows the Rio Tejo is a scenic way to see the city. Guided bike tours are another possibility. Cobbles and hills make cycling in the centre a slog at times.

Lisbon Neighbourhoods

Worth a Trip

⊙ Top Sights

Tram 28

Museu Nacional do Azulejo

Palácio Nacional de Sintra

Marquês de Pombal, Rato & Saldanha (p98)
Top-drawer museums, pristine gardens and some of Lisbon's best restaurants lure you north to these lesser-known neighbourhoods.

⊙ Top Sights

Museu Calouste Gulbenkian

Estrela, Lapa & Alcântara (p110)
A world-class ancient art museum, streets with low-key, leafy charm and dockside nightlife entice in these neighbourhoods.

⊙ Top Sights

Museu Nacional de Arte Antiga

Belém (p76)
Manueline monuments, a Unesco-listed monastery and contemporary art await in this nautical-flavoured neighbourhood by the river.

⊙ Top Sights

Mosteiro dos Jerónimos

Museu Colecção Berardo

Museu Nacional de Arte Antiga ⊙

Mosteiro dos Jerónimos ⊙

Museu Colecção Berardo ⊙

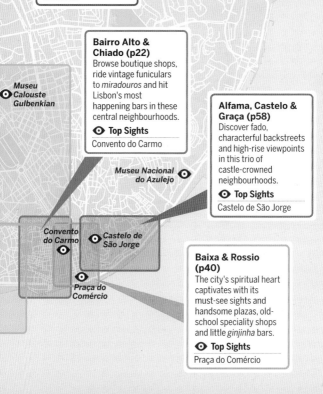

Parque das Nações (p88)

This riverside district shines with outdoor art, futuristic architecture and Europe's second-biggest aquarium.

◉ Top Sights

Oceanário

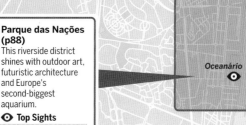

Oceanário
◉

Bairro Alto & Chiado (p22)

Browse boutique shops, ride vintage funiculars to *miradouros* and hit Lisbon's most happening bars in these central neighbourhoods.

◉ Top Sights

Convento do Carmo

Museu
◉ Calouste
Gulbenkian

Museu Nacional ◉
do Azulejo

Alfama, Castelo & Graça (p58)

Discover fado, characterful backstreets and high-rise viewpoints in this trio of castle-crowned neighbourhoods.

◉ Top Sights

Castelo de São Jorge

Convento
do Carmo
◉

◉ Castelo de
São Jorge

◉
Praça do
Comércio

Baixa & Rossio (p40)

The city's spiritual heart captivates with its must-see sights and handsome plazas, old-school speciality shops and little *ginjinha* bars.

◉ Top Sights

Praça do Comércio

Explore
Lisbon

Worth a Trip

A vintage tram arriving at Largo das Portas do Sol (p63)
RASPU/GETTY IMAGES ©

Explore

Bairro Alto & Chiado

Two neighbourhoods, two very different personalities. Chiado invites days spent boutique-shopping, gallery-hopping and lingering in literary cafes. Its more rakish, party-loving neighbour is Bairro Alto, a tangle of lanes harbouring dozens of shabby-chic shops, late-night bistros and hole-in-the-wall bars. Swinging south, Cais do Sodré has reinvented itself from red-light district to nightlife hub.

JOE DANIEL PRICE/GETTY IMAGES ©

The Sights in a Day

☀ Glide up the hillside, as folk have done since 1885, on the vintage **Elevador da Glória** (p30), pausing for castle-crowned city views from **Miradouro de São Pedro de Alcântara** (p30) at the top. Take a peek inside the opulently *azulejo*-clad **Igreja & Museu São Roque** (p30) before ambling downhill to Chiado. Factor in a little boutique-shopping and a creative lunch at the story-book-themed **Fábulas** (p33).

☀ Cultural afternoon? The **Convento do Carmo** (p24) presents a romp through the city's history with its entrancing ruins and stash of archaeological finds. Then make your way down to the river, stopping at the **Museu do Chiado** (p30) to contemplate works by Rodin and Jorge Vieira. It's a stiff hike or a quick ride on the **Elevador da Bica** (p31) to **Miradouro de Santa Catarina** (p31), where Lisbon spreads out photogenically before you. Enjoy those same views over a sundowner at **Noobai Café** (p34).

☾ Stay in Santa Catarina for a doctor's-orders dinner at pharmacy-themed **Pharmacia** (p32), or venture uphill to Bairro Alto for *petiscos* (tapas) and Portuguese wines at **Grapes & Bites** (p31). Take your pick of Bairro's pulsating bars and clubs.

For an evening out in Cais do Sodré, see p26.

👁 Top Sights
Convento do Carmo (p24)

🔍 Local Life
Cais do Sodré Bar Crawl (p26)

💜 Best of Lisbon
Bars & Nightlife
Park (p34)
Noobai Café (p34)
Pensão Amor (p27)

Food
Belcanto (p33)
Fumeiro de Santa Catarina (p31)
Grapes & Bites (p31)

Viewpoints
Miradouro de São Pedro de Alcântara (p30)

Getting There

Ⓜ **Metro** The green and blue lines stop at Baixa-Chiado; the green line runs to Cais do Sodré.

🚋 **Tram** Trams 15 and 18 stop at Cais do Sodré and tram 25 at Rua de São Paulo. Tram 28 is convenient for Santa Catarina.

🚌 **Bus** Bus 758 (Cais do Sodré–Benfica) stops at the Elevador da Glória and Príncipe Real.

Top Sights
Convento do Carmo

Soaring ethereally above Lisbon, the Convento do Carmo, founded as a convent for the Carmelite Order in 1389, was all but devoured by the 1755 earthquake. Its shattered pillars and wishbone-like arches are completely exposed to the elements. The Gothic nave collapsed on worshippers when the earthquake struck on All Saints' Day in 1755. The 19th-century taste for romantic ruins meant it was never restored as planned, and it later became the captivating archaeology museum you see today.

◉ Map p28, E4

Largo do Carmo

adult/child €3.50/free

🕙 10am-7pm Mon-Sat

Don't Miss

Nave

Open to the sky, the nave is scattered with evocative tombstones, statues, baptismal fonts and coats of arms. Look for the Renaissance loggia from Santarém, the Manueline window from the Mosteiro dos Jerónimos, 6th-century Hebraic funerary stelae and the baroque statue of St John Nepomucene from the old Alcântara bridge.

Main Chapel

First up in the archaeology museum is the main chapel, decorated with three baroque *azulejo* (tile) panels. It shelters the tomb of Nuno Álvares Pereira, who had the convent built to trumpet Portuguese victory in the 1385 Battle of Aljubarrota, alongside the early 14th-century tomb of Fernão Sanches, vividly depicting a boar hunt.

Pre-Columbian Treasures

Aztec statues, Chimu ceramics, Inca zoomorphic pottery and a trio of mummies – one battered Egyptian and two gruesome 16th-century Peruvians – are on display in room 4. The blue-and-white *azulejos* depict scenes from the Passion of Christ.

Roman-Moorish Collection

Roman milestones, funerary stelae and sarcophagi are showcased alongside later finds like a 6th-century Visigothic belt buckle in room 2. Two pillars adorned with griffins and a lion frieze are among the medieval Moorish standouts.

Prehistoric Finds

In room 1 you can zip back to prehistoric times contemplating Palaeolithic hand axes, Neolithic pottery, Megalithic tomb objects and Chalcolithic artefacts like loom weights.

☑ Top Tips

▶ Pick up a free map at the entrance to pinpoint the key exhibits.

▶ For the best photographs of the Convento do Carmo perched on the hillside, head down to Rossio.

▶ Don't miss the stunning view of Lisbon and Castelo de São Jorge from the museum shop.

✘ Take a Break

Sip a drink under the jacaranda trees on Largo do Carmo or try the nearby **Royale Café** (☏ 213 469 125; Largo Rafael Bordalo Pinheiro 29, Chiado; mains €8.50-11.50; ⊙11am-midnight Mon-Sat, 11am-8pm Sun) for creative sandwiches and shakes in a vine-clad courtyard.

Revive over pastries, *tartines* (open sandwiches) and lunch specials at **Tartine** (Rua Serpa Pinto 15; mains €7-9.50; ⊙8am-8pm Mon-Fri, 10am-8pm Sat; 🛜), a couple of minutes' stroll away.

Local Life
Cais do Sodré Bar Crawl

For years, riverside Cais do Sodré's backstreets were the haunt of whisky-slugging sailors craving after-dark sleaze. Then, in late 2011, the district went from seedy to stylish. Rua Nova do Carvalho was painted pink and the call girls were sent packing, but the edginess and decadence on which Lisbon thrives remains. Now party central, its boho bars, live-music venues and burlesque clubs are perfect for a late-night bar crawl.

❶ Tati Time

Begin an evening in mellow fashion at **Cafe Tati** (📞 213 461 279; www.cafetati. blogspot.com; Rua da Ribeira Nova 36; mains €7-8; 🕐 11am-1am Tue-Sun ; 🛜), which has undeniable charm amid its smattering of well-lit stone-arched rooms with stencilled walls. Live jazz and jam sessions, held several nights a week, bring in a party-loving, alternative crowd.

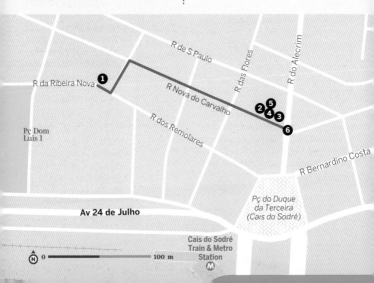

❷ Tinned Fish Tapas

You do not need much imagination to see what **Sol e Pesca** (Rua Nova do Carvalho 44; tinned fish around €3; ☺noon-4am) once was. Rods, nets, hooks and fish charts give away the tiny bar's former life as a fishing-tackle shop. Cabinets are stacked with vintage-looking cans of sardines, tuna and other tinned seafood, or '*conservas*' as the Portuguese say. Grab a chair, order a tin or two, and accompany it with bread, olives, wine and good company.

❸ Rising Fado Stars

When it comes to fado, it can be hard to find the real deal. Well, **Povo** (Rua Nova do Carvalho 32; small plates €4-8; ☺noon-2am Tue-Sat, 6pm-1am Sun & Mon) is it. A different *fadista* (fado singer) is in residence every month, there is no stage, *petiscos* (tapas) are served, and the aim is to give young, little-known singers exposure. The fado stars of tomorrow? Hear them here first.

❹ Bordello Chic

If the name **Pensão Amor** (www.pensaoamor.pt; Rua Nova do Carvalho 36; ☺noon-3am Mon-Wed, noon-4am Thu-Sat) doesn't give the game away, the graffiti murals of cavorting nudes and the scarlet walls surely will. A brothel reborn as an art space, it has a bordello-chic bar serving drinks and ceviche, a bookshop with erotic literature, and boutiques selling lingerie and vintage garb. Concerts, DJ sessions, plays and poetry recitals attract the crowds. Expect to queue at the weekend – it's worth the wait.

❺ Life is a Cabaret

Downstairs from Pensão Amor, the fabulously burlesque **Bar da Velha Senhora** (Rua Nova do Carvalho 40; ☺6pm-4am Tue-Sat), with its low-lit interior and glittering revue shows, whisks you back to those crazy cabaret days of the early 20th century. Tapas and cocktails with risqué names – don't ask, they made us blush – get the crowd in the mood for fado, cabaret, erotic poetry recitals and pianists bashing out songs like in the good old days.

❻ Gigs under the Bridge

Tucked under the arches of a bridge, the cavelike **Music Box** (www.musicboxlisboa.com; Rua Nova do Carvalho 24; ☺11pm-6am Mon-Sat) is all about the music. This is hands down one of the city's best venues for gigs, and you rarely pay more than €15 for a ticket. Concerts cover the entire spectrum, from jazz to indie and rock to metal, and DJs take over when the bands finish.

ROSSIO

R de Áurea

Pç Dom
Pedro IV
(Rossio)

R do Carmo

Cç do
Sacramento

Baixa-
Chiado

R 1 de Dezembro

Cç do Carmo

Lg do
Carmo

CHIADO

R do Duque

R da Condessa

Convento do Carmo &
Museu Arqueológico   34

R das Portas de Santo Antão

Pç dos
Restauradores

Estação do Rossio
(Rossio Train Station)

R da Oliveira

R da Trindade

Lg Rafael
Bordalo
Pinheiro   30

R. Jardim do
Regedor

R dos
Condes

Cç do Duque

R Nova da Trindade

27

26

Av da Liberdade

Restauradores

Cç da Glória

Elevador da Glória

Igreja & Museu
São Roque

4

Lg Trindade
Coelho

R da Misericórdia

31

Parque
Eduardo
VII

Miradouro de
São Pedro de
Alcântara

3

R do Norte

8

1

Tv da Boa Hora

Alcântara

R das Gáveas

R da Glória

R São Pedro de

R do Diário de Notícias

R da Taipas

R do Grémio
Lusitano

R da Barroca

21

R das Salgadeiras

R da Conceição da Glória

R das Taipas

Tv de São Pedro

R do Teixeira

12

15

R dos Mouros

Tv da Água da Flor

Tv da Queimada

R da Atalaia

22

R Luísa Todi

13

23

25

28

R da Rosa

R da Rosa

R Dom Pedro V

20

Cç do Tijolo

BAIRRO
ALTO

R do Século

R do Século

Tv dos Fiéis de Deus

18

Jardim
Botânico

Pç do
Príncipe
Real

R Eduardo Coelho

R Academia Ciências

Cç do Combro

PRÍNCIPE
REAL

R da Escola
Politécnica

Lg de
Jesus

R Luz Soriano

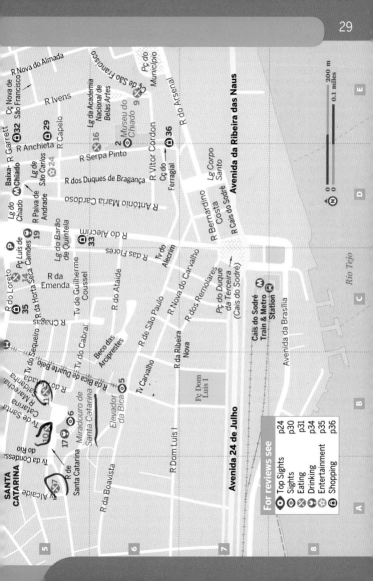

Sights

Miradouro de São Pedro de Alcântara

VIEWPOINT

1 Map p28, C2

Hitch a ride on the vintage Elevador da Glória from Praça dos Restauradores, or huff your way up steep Calçada da Glória to this terrific hilltop viewpoint. Fountains and Greek busts add a regal air to the surroundings, and the open-air cafe doles out wine, beer and snacks, which you can enjoy while taking in the castle views. (Rua São Pedro de Alcântara; ⏱viewpoint 24hr, cafe 10am-midnight Mon-Wed, to 2am Thu-Sun)

Local Life
Biking the Tejo

With its steep, winding hills and narrow, traffic-filled lanes, Lisbon may not seem like the ideal place to hop on a bicycle. However, the city is redefining itself with the addition of a new biking/jogging path. Coursing along the Rio Tejo for nearly 7km, the path connects Cais do Sodré with Belém, passing a rapidly changing landscape of ageing warehouses being converted into open-air cafes, restaurants and nightspots. You can rent wheels at **Bike Iberia** (Map 28, D7; ☎213 470 347; www.bike-iberia.com; Largo Corpo Santo 5; bike hire per 2hr/day from €7.50/14; ⏱9.30am-5pm) near Cais do Sodré.

Museu do Chiado

MUSEUM

2 Map p28, E6

Contemporary art fans flock to the Museu do Chiado, housed in the strikingly converted Convento de São Francisco. Temporary exhibitions lean toward interactive multimedia installations, while the gallery's permanent collection of 19th- and 20th-century works features pieces by Rodin, Jorge Vieira and José de Almada Negreiros. Revive over coffee in the small sculpture garden. (www.museuartecontemporanea.pt; Rua Serpa Pinto 4; adult/child €4.50/free, 1st Sun of the month free; ⏱10am-6pm Tue-Sun)

Elevador da Glória

FUNICULAR

3 Map p28, C3

Lisbon's second-oldest funicular has been shuttling folk from Praça dos Restauradores to Rua São Pedro de Alcântara since 1885. Knockout views await at the top. (Calçada da Glória; return €3.60; ⏱7am-midnight Mon-Thu, 7am-12.30pm Fri, 8.30am-12.30am Sat, 9am-midnight Sun)

Igreja & Museu São Roque

CHURCH, MUSEUM

4 Map p28, D3

The plain facade of 16th-century Jesuit Igreja de São Roque belies its dazzling interior of gold, marble and Florentine *azulejos* – bankrolled by Brazilian riches. Its star attraction is **Capela de São João Baptista**, a lavish confection of amethyst, alabaster, lapis lazuli and Carrara marble. The museum adjoining the church is packed with elaborate sacred art and holy relics. (Largo Trindade Coelho; church free, museum adult/child €2.50/free, free 10am-2pm Sun; ⏰church 2-7pm Mon, 9am-7pm Tue-Wed & Fri-Sun, 10am-8pm Thu, museum 2-7pm Mon, 10am-7pm Tue-Wed & Fri-Sun, 10am-8pm Thu)

Elevador da Bica

FUNICULAR

5 ⊙ Map p28, B6

This funicular has been creaking arthritically up the steep, narrow Rua da Bica de Duarte Belo since 1892. Jump aboard to save your legs and enjoy fleeting glimpses of the Rio Tejo and pastel-hued houses. (Rua de São Paulo; return trip €3.60; ⏰7am-9pm Mon-Sat, 9am-9pm Sun)

✓ Miradouro de Santa Catarina

VIEWPOINT

6 ⊙ Map p28, B5

Students bashing out rhythms, pot-smoking hippies, stroller-pushing parents and loved-up couples – all meet at this precipitous viewpoint in boho Santa Catarina. The views are fantastic, stretching from the river to the Ponte 25 de Abril and Cristo Rei. (Rua de Santa Catarina; admission free; ⏰24hr)

Eating

Fumeiro de Santa Catarina

TAPAS €

7 🍴 Map p28, A5

This nouveau-rustic tapas bar is a welcome newcomer to Santa Catarina's

AMEL JEAN-CLAUDE/GETTY IMAGES ©

Lemon sardines *petiscos* (tapas)

dining scene. Its menu of appetising *petiscos* focuses on smoked meat and fish – from confit of *bacalhau* (dried salt-cod) to beans with *chouriço* (spicy sausage). (📞213 471 002; Travessa do Alcaide 4C; tapas €2-8; ⏰7pm-12.30am Tue-Sat)

✗ Grapes & Bites

TAPAS €

8 🍴 Map p28, C4

The concept is simple: take a cosy den of a wine bar, kit it out with barrel tables, add live music and a fun crowd. Next, match a huge selection of Portuguese wines with *petiscos* like lemony sardines and Azeitão cheese. It's a winner. (📞919 361 171; Rua do Norte 81; mixed tapas around €15; ⏰2pm-2am)

Local Life
Have Your Cake

Lisbon has one seriously sweet tooth and nearly every corner has a *pastelaria* (pastry shop). Join locals for butter-rich rock cakes and custard tarts at old-school **Pastelaria São Roque** (Rua Dom Pedro V; pastries €1-3; ⏱7am-7pm), festooned with naturalistic *azulejos* (hand-painted tiles). Housed in a revamped butter factor, **Manteigaria** (Rua do Loreto 2; pastel de nata €1; ⏱8am-midnight) hits the mark with its superb *pastéis de nata* – crisp tarts that flake just so, filled with luscious custard and served with good strong coffee.

Tagide Wine & Tapas Bar

FUSION €€

9 🍴 Map p28, E6

Not to be confused with the pricier Tagide next door, this casual, slickly modern tapas bar has pretty views to the river. Small sharing plates are imaginative and packed with flavour. Three-course lunch specials, which include a glass of wine and coffee, cost €12.50. (☎213 404 010; Largo da Academia Nacional de Belas Artes 20; tapas €4-9; ⏱12.30-3pm & 7pm-midnight Tue-Thu, 12.30-3pm & 7pm-1am Fri, 2pm-1am Sat)

Pharmacia

MEDITERRANEAN €€

10 🍴 Map p28, B5

In Lisbon's apothecary museum, this wonderfully quirky restaurant dispenses tasting menus and tapas that sing with flavours that are both market fresh and Mediterranean influenced. Appetisers served in test tubes, and cabinets brimming with pill bottles and flacons – it's all part of the pharmaceutical fun. The terrace is a great spot for cocktails. (☎213 462 146; Rua Marechal Saldanha 2; tapas €7-11; ⏱1pm-1am Tue-Sun)

Le Petit Bistro

FUSION €€

11 🍴 Map p28, B5

On a lively stretch of Bica, the bohemian Petit Bistro serves both tapas-size plates and heartier mains from France and beyond (duck confit, gazpacho, wraps, lasagna, couscous dishes, hummus with bruschetta). Good late brunches (from 1pm) on weekends. (☎213 461 376; Rua do Almada 31; mains €9-14; ⏱7pm-midnight Wed-Fri, 1-4pm & 7pm-midnight Sat & Sun)

Decadente

PORTUGUESE €€

12 🍴 Map p28, C2

This beautifully designed restaurant, with touches of industrial chic, geometric artwork and an enticing back patio, dishes up inventive dishes showcasing high-end Portuguese ingredients at excellent prices. The changing three-course lunch menu (€10) is first-rate. Start off with creative cocktails in the front bar. (☎213 461 381; www.thedecadente.pt; Rua de São Pedro de Alcântara 81; mains €8-14; ⏱noon-3pm & 8-11pm Mon-Fri, 12.30-4pm & 8pm-midnight Sat, 8-11pm Sun)

Flor da Laranja

MOROCCAN €€

13 Map p28, C2

A great place to linger over a meal, Flor da Laranja earns rave reviews for its warm welcome, cosy ambience and delicious Moroccan cuisine. Top picks include dolmas, mouth-watering couscous dishes, lamb tagine, and fresh berry crêpes. (☑213 422 996; Rua da Rosa 206; mains €14-16; ☺7-11.30pm Mon-Sat)

Sea Me

SEAFOOD €€€

14 Map p28, C5

This urban-cool space serves up grilled fish by the kilo (check out the tempting fresh selection in the back), sushi and dishes with international accents – risotto with shrimp, Thai green curry with salmon, seared scallops with mango relish, and ceviche among other standouts. (☑213 461 564; www.peixaria-moderna.com; Rua do Loreto 21; mains €17-28; ☺12.30-3.30pm & 7.30pm-midnight Mon-Fri, 12.30pm-1am Sat, 12.30pm-midnight Sun)

100 Maneiras

FUSION €€€

15 Map p28, C2

How do we love 100 Maneiras? Let us count the hundred ways... The 10-course tasting menu changes daily and features imaginative, delicately prepared dishes. The courses are all a surprise – part of the charm – though the chef will take special diets and food allergies into consideration. There's a lively buzz to the elegant and small space. Reservations essential. (☑910 307 575; www.restaurante100maneiras.com; Rua do Teixeira 35; tasting menu €55, with wine pairing €90; ☺7.30pm-2am)

Belcanto

PORTUGUESE €€€

16 Map p28, D6

Shining brighter than any other Lisbon restaurant with two Michelin stars, José Avillez' Belcanto wows diners with its well-edited, creative menu, polished service and first-rate sommelier. Signatures like sea bass with seaweed and bivalves, and rosemary-smoked beef loin with bone marrow and garlic purée elevate Portuguese to a whole new level. Reservations are essential. (☑213 420 607; Largo de São Carlos 10; mains €42, tasting menu €90-145, two-/three-course lunch €45/60; ☺12.30-3pm & 7.30-11pm Tue-Sat)

Local Life
Coffee Culture

Bairro Alto and Chiado have a crop of boho-flavoured cafes good for whiling away an afternoon or evening. At the wonderfully relaxed **Fábulas** (Map p28, E5; Calçada Nova de São Francisco 14; mains €10-15, lunch specials €6-7; ☺10am-midnight; 🛜🖉) exposed stone, cosy nooks and flickering candles conjure a *fábula* (story-book fable). For drinks and light bites with knockout views of the castle and downtown Lisbon, head to the Indo-chic terrace at **Lost In** (Map p28, C2; Rua Dom Pedro V 56; ☺4pm-midnight Mon, 12.30pm-midnight Tue-Sat), shaded by colourful parasols.

Drinking

Noobai Café   BAR

17 🚇 Map p28, B5

Great views, winning cocktails and a festive crowd make Noobai a popular draw for a sundowner. Though it's next to Miradouro de Santa Catarina (p31), most people don't realise this bar is here until they descend the steps and a terrace unfurls before them. The vibe is laid-back, the music is funky jazz and the views over the Tejo are magical. (Miradouro de Santa Catarina; ⏰noon-midnight)

Park   BAR

18 🚇 Map p28, B4

If only all multi-storey car parks were like this... Climb up to the top floor, which has been transformed into one of Lisbon's hippest rooftop bars, with sweeping views reaching right down to the Tejo. The vibe is cool and creative. DJs spin jazz and house, and there are occasionally open-air cinema nights. (Calçada do Combro 58; ⏰1pm-2am Tue-Sat, 1-8pm Sun)

Bairro Alto Hotel   BAR

19 🚇 Map p28, D5

Rise in the gold-mesh lift to the 6th floor of Bairro Alto Hotel for sundowners and dazzling views over the rooftops to the river. It's a smart, grown-up lounge for cocktails and conversation as Lisbon starts to sparkle. (📞213 408 288; Praça Luís de Camões 2; ⏰11am-1.30am)

Pavilhão Chinês   BAR

20 🚇 Map p28, B2

Pavilhão Chinês is an old curiosity shop of a bar with oil paintings and model Spitfires dangling from the ceiling, and cabinets brimming with glittering Venetian masks and Action Men. Play pool or bag a comfy arm-

---

Understand
Bairro Alto

For years, working-class Bairro Alto was the place to throw off your Salazar straitjacket and indulge in a little after-dark sleaze. But while call girls no longer prowl these alleyways, the libertine lives on: graffitied slums have morphed into shabby-chic boutiques, alternative arts venues, tiny bistros, bars and clubs. It's lacklustre and as dead as a disused theatre by day; come twilight the nocturnal hedonist rears its sleepy head. Lanterns are flicked on, shutters raised and taxi drivers hurtle through the grid of narrow lanes.

For the real spirit of Bairro Alto, take the lead of locals: move from one bar to the next as the mood and music takes you; head out onto the cobbles to toast new-found friendships with €1 beers; live for the night.

chair to nurse a port or beer. Prices are higher than elsewhere, but such classy kitsch doesn't come cheap. (Rua Dom Pedro V 89-91; ⊘6pm-2am)

Artis   WINE BAR

21 🍷 Map p28, C3

Down a few steps from street level, Artis is a warmly lit place with old wood details, a jazzy soundtrack and an excellent selection of wines by the glass or bottle. Nicely turned out *petiscos* add to the appeal, with Galician-style octopus, flambéed Portuguese sausage and mixed cheese platters. (Rua Diário de Notícias 95; ⊘5.30pm-2am Sun & Tue-Thu, 5.30pm-3am Fri & Sat)

Capela   BAR

22 🍷 Map p28, C4

Once a Gothic chapel, today Capela's gospel is an experimental line-up of electronica and funky house. Get there early (before midnight) to appreciate the DJs before the crowds descend. Frescos, Renaissance-style nude murals and dusty chandeliers add a boho-chic touch. (Rua da Atalaia 45; ⊘8pm-2am Sun-Thu, 8pm-3am Fri-Sat)

Portas Largas   BAR

23 🍷 Map p28, C3

This Bairro Alto linchpin retains original fittings including black-and-white tiles, columns and porticos. It throws open *portas largas* (wide doors) to a mishmash of gays, straights and not-sures, who spill onto the cobbles with

PAUL BERNHARDT/GETTY IMAGES ©

Patrons outside a bar in Bairro Alto

zingy *caipirinhas*. Live bands most weekends. (Rua da Atalaia 105; ⊘8pm-2am)

Entertainment

Teatro Nacional de São Carlos   THEATRE

24 ⭐ Map p28, D5

Worth visiting just to see the sublime gold-and-red interior, this theatre has opera, ballet and theatre seasons. The summertime **Festival ao Largo** (www.festivalaolargo.pt; Largo de São Carlos) features free outdoor concerts on the plaza facing the theatre. (📞213 253 045; www.saocarlos.pt; Rua Serpa Pinto 9)

Zé dos Bois
LIVE MUSIC

25 ⭐ Map p28, C4

Focusing on tomorrow's performing arts and music trends, Zé dos Bois is an experimental venue with a graffitied courtyard, and an eclectic line-up of theatre, film, visual arts and live music. (www.zedosbois.org; Rua da Barroca 59; ⏰7pm-2am)

Fado in Chiado
FADO

26 ⭐ Map p28, D4

Inside a small theatre, the 50-minute nightly shows feature high-quality fado – a male and a female singer and two guitarists – and it is held early so you can grab dinner afterwards. (📞961 717 778; Espaço Chiado, Rua da Miséricordia 14; admission €17; ⏰7pm Mon-Sat)

Teatro da Trindade
THEATRE

27 ⭐ Map p28, D4

This early 20th-century gem stages an assortment of national and foreign productions. (📞213 420 000; www.teatro-trindade.inatel.pt; Largo da Trindade 7)

Mascote de Atalaia
FADO

28 ⭐ Map p28, C4

Petiscos (tapas), *vinho* (wine) and live fado keep the good vibes flowing at this intimate little bar. (Rua da Atalaia 13-15; ⏰5pm-2am Mon-Thu, 5pm-3am Fri & Sat)

Shopping

A Vida Portuguesa
GIFTS

29 🔒 Map p28, E5

A flashback to the late 19th century with its high ceilings and polished cabinets, this former warehouse and perfume factory lures nostalgics with all-Portuguese products, from retro-wrapped Tricona sardines to Claus Porto soaps, heart-embellished Viana do Castelo embroideries to Bordallo Pinheiro porcelain swallows. (Rua Anchieta 11; ⏰10am-8pm Mon-Sat, from 11am Sun)

Louie Louie
MUSIC

30 🔒 Map p28, D4

Clued-up DJs head for this funky music store stocking secondhand vinyl and

---

⃝ Local Life
Shop 'n' Stroll

Chiado's well-heeled **Rua do Carmo** is a catwalk to posh jewellers and designer names like Ana Salazar, while **Rua Garrett** is peppered with bookshops and speciality shops selling top-quality chocolate, coffee and more. For a more local scene, head to **Rua Dom Pedro V** and **Príncipe Real**, where you'll find the creations of up-and-coming Portuguese designers and antique, *azulejo* (tile) and interior-design shops. Late-night shoppers hit Bairro Alto, where hole-in-the-wall boutiques and concept stores sell everything from vintage garb, glitzy club wear and limited-edition Adidas to cork art, ceramics and vinyl. **Rua do Diário de Notícias**, **Rua das Salgadeiras** and **Rua do Norte** are also worth a mosey.

the latest house, dance and electronica grooves. Its tiny cafe does a mean chocolate cake. (Rua Nova da Trinidade 8; ⏱11am-7.30pm Mon-Sat, 3-7.30pm Sun)

A Carioca   FOOD

31 🔒 Map p28, D4

Little has changed since this old-world store opened in 1924: brass fittings still gleam, the coffee roaster is still in action and home blends, sugared almonds and toffees are still lovingly wrapped in green paper. (Rua da Misericórdia 9; ⏱9am-7pm Mon-Fri, to 1pm Sat)

Livraria Bertrand   BOOKS

32 🔒 Map p28, E5

Amid 18th-century charm Bertrand has excellent selections, including titles in English, French and Spanish. (Rua Garrett 73; ⏱9am-10pm Mon-Sat, 11am-8pm Sun)

Fábrica Sant'Ana ✓   HANDICRAFTS

33 🔒 Map p28, D5

Hand-making and painting *azulejos* since 1741, this is the place to get some eye-catching porcelain tiles for your home. (Rua do Alecrim 95; ⏱9.30am-7pm Mon-Fri, 10am-7pm Sat)

Luvaria Ulisses   CLOTHING

34 🔒 Map p28, E4

So tiny it's almost an optical illusion, this magical art-deco store is chock-full of soft handmade leather gloves in kaleidoscope shades. (Rua do Carmo 87A; ⏱10am-7pm Mon-Sat)

🔍 Local Life
Mercado da Ribeira

Doing trade in fresh fruit and veg, fish and flowers since 1892, the **Mercado da Ribeira** (Avenida 24 de Julho; ⏱10am-midnight Sun-Wed, 10am-2am Thu-Sat) is the word on everyone's lips since Time Out transformed half of it into a gourmet food court in 2014. Now it's like Lisbon in microcosm, with everything from Garrafeira Nacional wines to Conserveira de Lisboa fish, Arcádia chocolate and Santini gelato.

Follow the lead of locals and come for a morning mooch followed by lunch at one of 35 kiosks.

Vellas Loreto   CANDLES

35 🔒 Map p28, C5

Lisboetas have been waxing lyrical about this specialist candle-maker since 1789. The wood-panelled, talc-scented store sells myriad candles, from cherubs and peppers to Christmas trees and water lilies. (Rua do Loreto 53; ⏱9am-7pm Mon-Sat)

Story Tailors   CLOTHING

36 🔒 Map p28, E6

This chandelier-lit enchanted forest of fashion houses design duo Luís Sanchez and João Branco, who bewitch with fairy-tale dresses, floaty ruffle skirts, quirky reversible coats and their latest catwalk creations. (www.storytailors.pt; Calçada do Ferragial 8; ⏱noon-8pm Tue-Sat)

Local Life
Strolling Príncipe Real

1st
D AM

Getting There

🚌 **Bus** The 202 (Cais do Sodré–B.º Padre Cruz) and 758 (Cais do Sodré–Benfica) shuttle frequently between Praça do Príncipe Real and central stops like Praça Luís de Camões and Rato.

Wedged between Bairro Alto and Rato, Príncipe Real is an open-minded, bohemian-flavoured corner of Lisbon, perfect for lazy days spent exploring markets, antique stores and hip boutiques, or watching the world go by over coffee on a tree-shaded square. Artists, up-and-coming designers and the gay community all call this enclave home, giving it its creative, blissfully relaxed vibe.

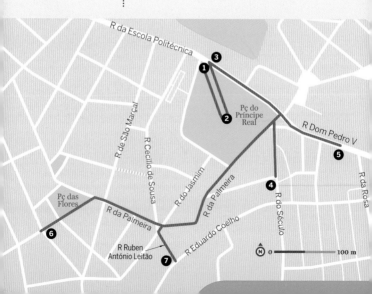

❶ Morning Coffee

Start your day in leisurely fashion at the **Esplanada** (📞962 311 669; Praça do Príncipe Real; light meals €5-11; 🕙9am-11pm Sun-Wed, 9am-2am Thu-Sat), a cafe with tables under the trees.

❷ Plaza Stroll

A century-old cedar tree forms a giant natural parasol at the centre of palm-dotted **Praça do Príncipe Real**, where Lisboetas from all walks of life hang out. The square is rimmed by elegant 19th-century townhouses; most striking of all is the powder-puff-pink **Palácio Ribeiro da Cunha** at No 26.

❸ Innovative Design ✗ NYT

If you want to find Lisbon's cutting edge, Praça do Príncipe Real is where it is currently at. Designers and creatives from the emerging to the established show their latest work at **21pr Concept Store** (Praça do Príncipe Real 21; 🕙10.30am-7.30pm Mon-Sat), the brainchild of fashion guru Ricardo Preto, and neo-Moorish **Embaixada** (www.embaixadalx.pt; Praça do Príncipe Real 26; 🕙noon-2am Thu-Sat, to midnight Sun-Wed).

❹ Deli Delight   Lunch!

Tucked down a side-street off the square is the **Mercearia do Século** (📞966 921 280; Rua de O Século 145; two-course lunch €9; 🕙9am-8pm Mon-Fri, 9am-9pm Sat). Anthropologist and Portuguese cookbook writer Fernanda runs this sweet little deli and grocery store with love and an eye for careful sourcing. <u>Lunch menus are whole</u>some and big on flavour. You can also stock up on foodie gifts – fig bread, preserves, honey, olive oil etc.

❺ Fashion Focus 🖊

Lisbon is no longer the wallflower of the international fashion scene. The city has carved out a reputation as a catwalk capital to watch, and nowhere is it reflected more than on hip strip Rua Dom Pedro V. Check out Lidija Kolovrat's boldly patterned wonders at **Kolovrat 79** (www.lidijakolovrat.org; Rua Dom Pedro V 79; 🕙11am-8pm Mon-Sat, 2-8pm Sun), the flagship store of clean-cut **Alex-andra Moura** (www.alexandramoura.com; Rua Dom Pedro V 77; 🕙11am-8pm Mon-Sat) and super-sleek boutique **Espaço B** (Rua Dom Pedro V 120; 🕙10.30am-7.30pm Mon-Sat).

❻ Cupcake O'Clock ◀

Just around the corner from pretty Praça das Flores, is **Tease** (Rua Nova da Piedade 15; cupcakes €2.50; 🕙11am-11pm Mon-Thu, 9am-midnight Fri & Sat, 10am-8pm Sun). This rock 'n' roll bakery churns out fabulous frosted cupcakes and freshly brewed teas. The decor includes a mosaic of exquisite *azulejos* (hand-painted tiles).

❼ Decadent Cocktails 🖊

For Lisbon's most creative cocktails, make your way to **Cinco Lounge** (www.cincolounge.com; Rua Ruben António Leitão 17; 🕙9pm-2am), where Dave Palethorpe works mixology magic. Chocolate sofas, candles and a kiss of gold make this slinky lounge ideal for sipping and conversing.

Explore

Baixa & Rossio

Built high and mighty on the rubble of the 1755 earthquake, Baixa is Lisbon's riverfront gateway, its royal flag-bearer, its lifeblood. Trams rumble, buskers hold crowds captive and shoppers mill around old-world stores. The main drag, Rua Augusta, links the regal Praça do Comércio to Rossio, where you'll find a neighbourly vibe in closet-sized *ginjinha* (cherry liqueur) bars and street cafes.

The Sights in a Day

☀ Wake up over a 360-degree city view at the top of the neo-Gothic **Elevador de Santa Justa** (p47) before the crowds arrive. Then meander south along Rua Augusta to the riverside **Praça do Comércio** (p42), Lisbon's spiritual and geographical heart with its vintage trams, grand arcades and general hustle-bustle. Go old-school shopping in the backstreets for cheese, port and tinned fish, as well as buttons and threads on haberdashery-fringed Rua da Conceição.

☀ Polish off one of the famous roast-pork sandwiches at **Nova Pombalina** (p50), saving room for creamy gelato at **Fragoleto** (p43). Fortified, take a whistle-stop tour of the design world at the free **Museu de Design e da Moda** (p49). As dusk sets in, head up to **Rossio** (p47) to see its fountains, theatre and neo-Manueline train station light up.

☾ Love it or loathe it, you have to try *ginjinha* and Rossio is the place for a sunset shot. Choose from the bistros lining the pedestrian Rua das Portas de Santo Antão or the castle-facing steps of Calçada do Duque for dinner. Afterwards, let Lisbon's skyline work its charms from the **Rooftop Bar** (p52) atop Hotel Mundial.

For a local's day in Baixa and Rossio, see p44.

👁 Top Sights
Praça do Comércio (p42)

🔍 Local Life
Baixa Back in Time (p44)

💗 Best of Lisbon

Bars & Nightlife
A Ginjinha (p52)

Contemporary Art & Design
Museu de Design e da Moda (p49)

Viewpoints
Rooftop Bar (p52)

Shopping
Conserveira de Lisboa (p45)

Tram & Funicular Rides
Elevador de Santa Justa (p47)

Getting There

Ⓜ **Metro** Baixa-Chiado, Rossio, Terreiro do Paço, Restauradores.

🚋 **Tram** Trams 12 (circular route) and 15 to Algés via Alcântara and Belém depart from Praça da Figueira. Trams 18 and 25 stop at Praça do Comércio: tram 18 en route to Ajuda via Alcântara, and tram 25 to Campo Ourique via Estrela. Pick up tram 28 at Martim Moniz or Rua Conceição.

JEAN-PIERRE LESCOURRET/GETTY IMAGES ©

Top Sights
Praça do Comércio

There's no place like Praça do Comércio for the 'wow, I'm in Lisbon!' effect. Everyone arriving by boat used to disembark here, and it still feels like the gateway to Lisbon, thronging with activity and trams. With its 18th-century arcades and triumphal arch, this is the city at its monumental best. Wander the riverfront, gaze up at the equestrian statue, and see the history of Lisbon mapped out in stone. This handsome plaza witnessed the worst of the 1755 earthquake and the fall of the monarchy in 1908, and lived to tell the tale.

Terreiro do Paço

Map p46, C5

Equestrian statue of Dom José I in Praça do Comércio

Don't Miss

Arco da Vitória

Built in the wake of the 1755 earthquake, this **triumphal arch** (Rua Augusta 2-10; admission €2.50) is a riot of columns crowned with allegorical figures representing Glory, Valour and Genius, and carried high by bigwigs including Vasco da Gama and Marquês de Pombal. A lift whisks you to the top, where fine views of Praça do Comércio, the river and the castle await.

Dom José I

The square's centrepiece, an 18th-century equestrian statue of the king Dom José I, hints at the square's royal roots as the pre-earthquake site of Palácio da Ribeira.

Riverfront

Praça do Comércio leads elegantly down to the banks of the Tejo. The riverfront promenade is a popular gathering spot, with its sweeping views, boat trips and buskers. Across the water you can glimpse the 110m-high Cristo Rei (p50).

ViniPortugal

Under the arcades, vaulted tasting room **ViniPortugal** (www.viniportugal.pt; ⏲11am-7pm Tue-Sat) is a viticultural organisation offering several wine tastings a day. A €2 enocard allows you to taste between two and four Portuguese wines, from Alentejo whites to full-bodied Duoro reds.

Pátio da Galé

Lisbon's showpiece, the Pátio da Galé, harbours the restored inner courtyard of the former royal palace. Following a huge makeover, the complex is home to the tourist office, Lisbon Shop (p55) and people-watching cafes and restaurants.

☑ **Top Tips**

▶ Come in the early morning to appreciate the square at its most peaceful and in the evening to see its monuments beautifully lit up.

▶ Tie in your visit with a tour – Praça do Comércio is the starting point for many boat excursions and city walks.

✗ **Take a Break**

Head to nearby **Fragoleto** (Map p46, C4; Rua da Prata 61; small/medium/large €2.20/3.50/5; ⏲11am-8pm;) for rich, creamy Italian-style gelato, in unusual flavours like goat's milk and chocolate, avocado and lemon with basil.

The pick of the restaurants facing Lisbon's biggest plaza, **Can the Can** (Map p46, C5 218 851 392; Praça do Comércio 82; mains €10.50-20; ⏲9am-midnight) literally does what it says on the tin – paying homage to the humble canned fish in appetisers and sharing plates.

Local Life
Baixa Back in Time

Wandering the cobbled laneways of Baixa and Rossio is like time travel. Bee-yellow funiculars and trams rumble up steep inclines as they have since the late 19th century, shoeshiners ply their trade and specialty stores thrive. As you stroll, you will come across thimble-sized haberdasheries, old-world patisseries and cupboard-sized *ginjinha* bars that serve nostalgia in a shot glass.

....

❶ Mad Hatters
Lisbon's maddest hatters, **Azevedo Rua** (Praça Dom Pedro IV 73; ⏱10am-7pm Mon-Fri, to 2.30pm Sat) have been covering bald spots since 1886. Expect good old-fashioned service and wood-panelled cabinets full of tweedy flat caps, bonnets, straw hats, bowlers and Ascot-worthy headwear.

❷ Old-School Shop

Relive the days spent shopping with Gran on and around **Praça da Figueira** (Map p46, C2). Close by, century-old **Manteigaria Silva** (Rua Dom Antão de Almada 1D; ⏲9am-7.30pm) does a brisk trade in Portuguese ham, cheese, wine and *bacalhau* (dried salt-cod). The tiny **Antiga Casa do Bacalhau** (Praça da Figueira 2B; ⏲9am-7pm Mon-Fri, 9am-1pm Sat) weighs *bacalhau* on vintage scales and sells it by the kilo.

❸ Coffee & Cake

Since 1829, **Confeitaria Nacional** (Praça da Figueira 18; lunches €9-11; ⏲8am-8pm) patisserie has been expanding waist-lines with its egg and almond sweets, macaroons and *pastéis de nata* (custard tarts). Take a seat in the stuccoed interior for coffee and cake Lisbon-style.

❹ Portuguese Flavours

As you make your way back towards Rossio, stop off at **Manuel Tavares** (Rua da Betesga 1A; ⏲9.30am-7.30pm Mon-Sat), a beautiful wood-fronted shop that has been tempting locals since 1860 with *pata negra* (cured ham), pungent cheeses, *ginjinha* and other treats.

❺ Vintage Heaven

Vintage divas make for retro boutique **Outra Face da Lua** (Rua da Assunção 22; ⏲10am-8pm Mon-Sat, noon-7pm Sun; 📶), crammed with puffball dresses, lurex skirts and wildly patterned '70s shirts. Jazz and electronica play overhead. Revive over salads, sandwiches, cocktails and cosmic iced tea at the in-store cafe.

❻ Set in Stone

Easy on the eye, hard on the foot, Lisbon's mosaic cobblestones have been polished smooth over centuries. Keep an eye out for the **Calceteiro** on Rua da Vitória, a bronze statue of a paver, hammer in hand, which pays tribute to those who laid the city's many thousands of cobblestones.

❼ Buttons & Threads

With its cluster of dark-wood-panelled, closet-sized haberdasheries, **Rua da Conceição** recalls an era where folk still used to darn stockings. Buttons, ribbons, threads and trimmings line the walls in art-nouveau **Retrosaria Bijou** (Rua da Conceição 91; ⏲9.30am-7pm Mon-Fri, 8am-1pm Sat) and many others like it.

❽ Retro Tinned Fish

How apt that in Rua dos Bacalhoeiros ('cod-vessel street') lies 1930s shop **Conserveira de Lisboa** (Rua dos Bacalhoeiros 34; ⏲9am-7pm Mon-Sat), dedicated wholly to tinned fish, whose walls are a mosaic of retro wrappings. An elderly lady and her son tot up on a monstrous old till and wrap purchases in brown paper.

❾ Sundown Shots

Hipsters, old men in flat caps, office workers and tourists all meet at **A Ginjinha** (p52) for shots of *ginjinha*. Watch the owner line 'em up at the bar under the beady watch of the drink's 19th-century inventor, Espinheira, then join the crowds outside.

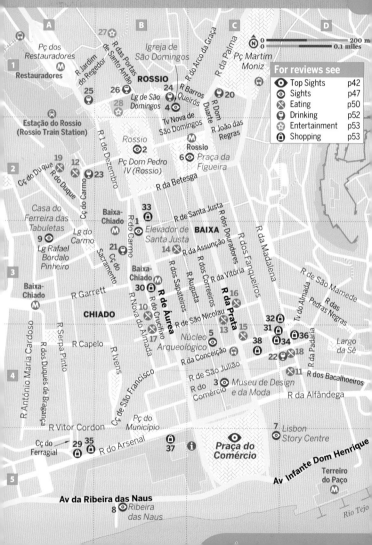

A

Pç dos
Restauradores

Restauradores Ⓜ

R Jardim
do Regedor

27 ✪

R das Portas
de Santo Antão

B

Igreja de
São Domingos

ROSSIO

R Barros
Queirós

25 Ⓐ

26 Ⓐ

28 ✪

Lg de São
Domingos

24 Ⓐ

4 Ⓐ

R do Arco da Graça

C

R da Palma

Pç Martim
Moniz

20 Ⓐ

R Dom
Duarte

D

N ⊙   0   200 m
         0   0.1 miles

For reviews see
👁 Top Sights   p42
👁 Sights   p47
✕ Eating   p50
🍷 Drinking   p52
✪ Entertainment p53
🔒 Shopping   p53

Estação do Rossio
(Rossio Train Station)

R 1 de Dezembro

Rossio

2 ⊙

Pç Dom Pedro
IV (Rossio)

Tv Nova de
São Domingos

Rossio Ⓜ

6 ⊙ *Praça da
Figueira*

R João das
Regras

19 Ⓐ 12 Ⓐ

Cç do Duque

R do Duque

23 Ⓐ

Cç do Carmo

R da Betesga

Casa do
Ferreira das
Tabuletas

33 Ⓐ

**Baixa-
Chiado** Ⓜ

R do Carmo

Elevador de
Santa Justa

BAIXA

R de Santa Justa

9 ⊙

Lg do
Carmo

Lg Rafael
Bordalo
Pinheiro

21 Ⓐ

R do Sacramento

Cç do Carmo

14 ✕

R da Assunção

R dos Dourados

R dos Fanqueiros

R da Madalena

R de São Mamede

R das
Pedras Negras

**Baixa-
Chiado** Ⓜ

**Baixa-
Chiado** Ⓜ

CHIADO

R Garrett

30 Ⓐ

1 Ⓐ

R de Áurea

R Nova do Almada

R dos Sapateiros

R dos Correeiros

R Augusta

R da Vitória

R da Prata

16 Ⓐ

Tv do Almada

R do Padaria

R de São Mamede

R Capelo

R Serpa Pinto

10 Ⓐ

17 ✕

R do Crucifixo

R de São Nicolau

*Núcleo
Arqueológico*

5 Ⓐ

13 Ⓐ

15 ✕

32 Ⓐ

31 Ⓐ 34 Ⓐ 36 Ⓐ

Largo
da Sé

R António Maria Cardoso

R dos Duques de Bragança

R Vitor Cordon

R Ivens

Cç de São Francisco

R da Conceição

38 Ⓐ

22 Ⓐ 18 Ⓐ

11 ✕

R dos Bacalhoeiros

R de São Julião

3 ⊙ *Museu de Design
e da Moda*

R da Alfândega

Cç do
Ferragial

29 Ⓐ 35 Ⓐ

R do Arsenal

Pç do
Município

R do
Comércio

37 Ⓐ

ⓘ

⊙ *Praça do
Comércio*

7 ⊙ *Lisbon
Story Centre*

Av Infante Dom Henrique

Terreiro
do Paço Ⓜ

Av da Ribeira das Naus

8 ⊙ *Ribeira
das Naus*

Rio Tejo

A fountain in Rossio (Praça Dom Pedro IV)

Sights

Elevador de Santa Justa

ELEVATOR

1 Map p46, B3

If the lanky, wrought-iron Elevador de Santa Justa seems uncannily familiar, it's probably because the neo-Gothic marvel is the handiwork of Raul Mésnier, Gustave Eiffel's apprentice. It's Lisbon's only vertical street lift. Get there early to beat the crowds and zoom to the top for sweeping views over the city's skyline. (cnr Rua de Santa Justa & Largo do Carmo; return trip €5; ☉7am-10.45pm)

Rossio

PLAZA

2 Map p46, B2

Simply Rossio to locals, Praça Dom Pedro IV has 24-hour buzz. Shoe-shiners and lottery ticket sellers, hash-peddlers and office workers drift across its wavelike cobbles, gazing up to its ornate fountains and **Dom Pedro IV** (Brazil's first emperor), perched high on a marble pedestal.

And these cobbles have seen it all: witch burnings and bullfights, rallies and 1974 revolution carnations. Don't miss **Estação do Rossio**, a frothy neo-Manueline station with horseshoe-shaped arches and swirly turrets. Trains depart here for Sintra. (Praça Dom Pedro IV)

Understand

The Earthquake that Shook Lisbon

The Fall of a Thriving City

Picture, if you can, Lisbon in its heyday: Portugal has discovered gold in Brazil; merchants are flocking to the city to trade in gold, spices, silks and jewels; the city is a magnificent canvas of 16th-century Manueline architecture. At the heart of it all is Baixa and the royal Palácio da Ribeira rising triumphantly above Terreiro do Paço square.

Now fast-forward to 9.40am on All Saints' Day, 1 November 1755: the day that everything changed. Three major earthquakes hit as residents celebrated Mass. The tremors brought an even more devastating fire and tsunami. Much of the city fell like a pack of dominoes, never to regain its former status; palaces, libraries, art galleries, churches and hospitals were razed to the ground. Some estimate that as many as 90,000 of Lisbon's 270,000 inhabitants died.

The Rise of Baixa & Pombaline Architecture

Enter the formidable, unflappable, geometrically minded Sebastião de Melo, better known as the Marquês de Pombal. As Dom João I's chief minister, the Marquês de Pombal swiftly set about reconstructing the city, good to his word to 'bury the dead and heal the living'. In the wake of the disaster, the autocratic statesman not only kept the country's head above water as it was plunged into economic chaos, but he also managed to propel Lisbon into the modern era.

Together with military engineers and architects Eugenio dos Santos and Manuel da Maia, the Marquês de Pombal played a pivotal role in reconstructing the city in a simple, cheap, earthquake-proof way that created today's formal grid, and Pombaline style was born. The antithesis of rococo, Pombaline architecture was functional and restrained: *azulejos* (hand-painted tiles) and decorative elements were used sparingly, building materials were prefabricated, and wide streets and broad plazas were preferred.

The best example of Pombaline style is the Baixa Pombalina, delineated by Rossio to the north and Praça do Comércio to the south. The neighbourhood has been on the Unesco list of tentative World Heritage Sites since 2004.

Museu de Design e da Moda
MUSEUM

3 Map p46, C4

Baixa's star is the Museum of Design and Fashion, a cavernous concrete-walled space – set in a former bank – that contains furniture, industrial design and couture dating from the 1930s to the present. Highlights include iconic furniture by Arne Jacobsen, Charles Eames and Frank Gehry, plus haute couture by the likes of Givenchy, Christian Dior and Balenciaga. (www.mude.pt; Rua Augusta 24; admission free; ⏰10am-6pm Tue-Sun)

Igreja de São Domingos
CHURCH

4 Map p46, B1

It's a miracle that this church still stands, having barely survived the 1755 earthquake, then fire in 1959. A sea of tea lights illuminates gashed pillars, battered walls and ethereal sculptures in its musty, yet enchanting, interior. Note the Star of David outside marking the spot of a bloody anti-Semitic massacre in 1506. (Largo de São Domingos; admission free; ⏰7.30am-7pm Mon-Fri, noon-6pm Sat)

Núcleo Arqueológico
RUINS

5 Map p46, C4

Hidden under Banco Comercial Portuguesa is the Núcleo Arqueológico, a web of tunnels believed to be the remnants of a Roman spa dating from the 1st century AD. You can descend into the depths on a fascinating guided tour in English (departing on the hour) run by the Museu da Cidade. (Rua Augusta 96; admission free; ⏰10am-6pm Mon-Sat)

Praça da Figueira
PLAZA

6 Map p46, C2

Praça da Figueira is framed by whizzing traffic, Pombaline townhouses and alfresco cafes with stellar views of hilltop Castelo de São Jorge. At its centre rises gallant King João I, once celebrated for his 15th-century discoveries in Africa, now targeted by pigeons and gravity-defying skateboarders.

Understand
Portuguese Inquisition

The neoclassical grandeur of of Teatro Nacional D Maria II evokes nothing of its sinister background as Palácio dos Estaus, seat of the Portuguese Inquisition from 1540. Those found guilty of heresy, witchcraft or practising Judaism were publicly executed on Praça Dom Pedro IV (Rossio) or Largo de São Domingos. Though King João III – o Piedoso (the Pious) – launched the Inquisition in 1536, the persecution of Jews goes back further; look for the Star of David in front of Igreja de São Domingos, which marks the spot of a bloody anti-Semitic massacre in 1506.

○ Local Life

Cristo Rei

Visible from almost anywhere in Lisbon, the 110m **Cristo Rei** (www. cristorei.pt; adult/child €4/2; ⊘9.30am-6pm) is a statue of Christ with outstretched arms. The slightly more baroque version of Rio de Janeiro's Christ the Redeemer was erected in 1959 to thank God for sparing Portugal from the horrors of WWII. A lift zooms you up to a platform, from where Lisbon spreads magnificently before you.

To reach Cristo Rei, take the breezy commuter ferry from Terreiro do Paço Ferry Terminal to the sleepy seaside suburb of Cacilhas (€1.20, 15 minutes), then bus 101.

Lisbon Story Centre   MUSEUM

7 ◎ Map p46, C5

This museum takes visitors on a 60-minute journey through Lisbon's history, from its early foundation (pre-Ancient Roman days) to modern times. An audio guide and multimedia exhibits describe key episodes, including New World discoveries, the terrifying 1755 earthquake (with a vivid film re-enacting the horrors) and the ambitious reconstruction that followed. (www.lisboastorycentre.pt; Praça do Comércio 78; adult/child €7/3; ⊘10am-8pm)

Ribeira das Naus   PROMENADE

8 ◎ Map p46, B5

Lisbon's recently regenerated waterfront revolves around this riverfront promenade between Praça do Comércio and Cais do Sodré. With broad views over the river, it's a fine place for strolling, lounging, reading, cycling and kicking back with a coffee at the kiosk. This is the closest Lisbon gets to an urban beach.

Casa do Ferreira das Tabuletas   HISTORIC BUILDING

9 ◎ Map p46, A3

The eye-catching Casa do Ferreira das Tabuletas dates to 1864. Its *trompe l'œil azulejos* (hand-painted tiles) depict allegorical figures and the elements. (Rua da Trindade 28-34)

Eating

A Palmeira   PORTUGUESE €

10 ✕ Map p46, B3

Popular among Baixa's lunching locals, A Palmeira dishes up good, honest Portuguese fare, from grilled fish to beef stew, in an old-fashioned tiled interior. Look for the palm on the sign. (Rua do Crucifixo 69; mains €7-10; ⊘11am-9pm Mon-Fri)

Nova Pombalina   PORTUGUESE €

11 ✕ Map p46, D4

The reason this bustling traditional restaurant is always packed around midday is its delicious *leitão* (suckling pig) sandwich, served on freshly baked bread in 60 seconds or less by the lightning-fast crew behind the counter. (Rua do Comércio 2; sandwiches €3.50; ⊘7am-7.30pm)

El Rei D'Frango
GRILL HOUSE €

12 Map p46, A2

Grill goddesses Luciana and Carla rustle up enormous and delicious portions of salmon and *febras* (sautéed pork strips) for pocket money. You'll *roll* down the cobbles after eating at this simple local haunt. (213 424 066; Calçada do Duque 5; dishes €6-8; noon-3.30pm & 7-10pm Mon-Sat)

Moma
FUSION €

13 Map p46, C3

A nice break from grilled sardines and menu-touting hawks in Baixa, this local haunt boasts black-and-white tile floors and a small but creative menu (spicy crispy prawns, pasta with wild mushrooms, and arugula salad with goat cheese and grilled eggplant are three recent favourites). (Rua de São Nicolau 47; mains €7.50-9; noon-6.30pm Mon-Fri)

Amorino
ICE CREAM €

14 Map p46, B3

Amorino serves the city's best gelato – rich decadence made from organic, high-quality ingredients. (Rua Augusta 209; small/large €3.50/5.50; 10.30am-11pm)

Nata
PATISSERIE €

15 Map p46, C4

'The World Needs Nata' is the strapline of this aptly named patisserie. And indeed the perfectly crisp *pastéis de nata* (custard tarts) that fly out of the oven here are spot-on. (Rua da Prata 78; pastéis de nata €1; 8am-8pm;)

Bebedouro
TAPAS €€

16 Map p46, C3

Wine-bottle lights illuminate stylish Bebedouro, where full-bodied Douro wines are nicely paired with tasting platters of regional cheese and sausage, bruschetti, creative salads and *petiscos* (tapas) like octopus in ragout and garlic potatoes. There's a good buzz, friendly service and a little pavement terrace. (Rua de São Nicolau 24; tapas €5-10; noon-11.45pm Wed-Mon)

Oito Dezoito
PORTUGUESE €€

17 Map p46, B4

It's named after the time it takes a sunray to reach the earth, and Oito Dezoito (Eight Eighteen) shines with its Italian-inspired cuisine. Clean lines and charcoal and cream tones create a sleek backdrop for brunch, lunch or dishes like tender roast lamb with

---

Top Tip

Free View

Panoramic though it is, the ride on the **Elevador de Santa Justa** is over in the blink of an eye. If you don't fancy the lift, you can enjoy the same view free from the entrance on Largo do Carmo. Here the whole of Lisbon spreads picturesquely before you: from Rossio and Chiado to Sé (cathedral) and Igreja de São Vicente de Fora. There's a cafe and snack bar at the top if you want to linger for a while.

pomegranate and chestnut sauce.
Wines are available by the glass. (☑961
330 226; www.oitodezoito.pt; Rua de São Nicolau 114; mains €12-20; ⏰noon-2am Mon-Sat)

Tasca Kome   JAPANESE €€

18 ✗ Map p46, D4

Hidden away on a Baixa backstreet,
this intimate *tasca* (tavern) serves
super-fresh Japanese food. Sushi,
sashimi, *shime saba* (mackerel ceviche)
and slow-cooked pork belly are nicely
washed down with sake or *mugi-cha*
(barley tea). (☑211 340 117; www.kome-
lisboa.com; Rua da Madalena 57; mains €8-16;
⏰noon-3pm & 7-10.30pm Tue-Sat)

Local Life
Ginjinha

Come dusk, the area around Largo
de São Domingos and the adjacent
Rua das Portas de Santo Antão
buzzes with locals getting their
cherry fix in a cluster of *ginjinha*
bars. **A Ginjinha** (Largo de Saõ Domingos 8; ⏰9am-10pm) is famous as the
birthplace of the sugary sweet tipple
thanks to a quaffing friar from Igreja
Santo Antonio who revealed the
secret to an entrepreneurial Galician
by the name of Espinheira. Nearby
are other postage-stamp-sized bars
to try. For little more than €1, you
can order a *ginjinha sem* (without)
or – our favourite – *com* (with) the
alcohol-soaked cherries. It's a fine
way to start or end your evening.

Café Buenos Aires   ARGENTINE €€€

19 ✗ Map p46, A2

Your taste buds will tango at this boho
Argentine gem, perched high on the
cobbled steps of Calçada do Duque.
Candles flicker, loved-up couples coo
and amigos tuck into Argentine steaks
and chocolate cake with *dulce de
leche* (caramel spread). (☑213 420 739;
Calçada do Duque 31; dishes €14-20)

Drinking

Rooftop Bar   BAR

20 🍷 Map p46, C1

Grab a table at sundown on the Hotel
Mundial's roof terrace for a sweeping
view of Lisbon and its hilltop castle.
Its backlit bar, white sofas and ambi-
ent sounds set the stage for evening
drinks and sharing plates. (Hotel Mundial, Praça Martim Moniz 2; ⏰6.30-12.30pm)

Liquid   JUICE BAR

21 🍷 Map p46, B3

Get juiced at this hole-in-the-wall bar,
with fresh-pressed juices (including
detox ones) and smoothies. (Rua Nova
do Almada 45A; ⏰9am-7pm Mon-Sat)

Bar Trobadores   BAR

22 🍷 Map p46, D4

In nightlife-starved Baixa, Bar
Trobadores harks back to the Middle
Ages with a candle-lit interior, solid
wood tables and low-hanging iron
chandeliers. There's live music most

weekends (minstral-inspired groups, Celtic, fado) and a good beer selection (including Duvel, Chimay and other Belgian brews). (Rua de São Julião 27; ⏱5pm-2am Sun-Thu, 5pm-4am Fri & Sat)

Ginjinha do Carmo   GINJINHA BAR

23 🍷 Map p46, A2

Tucked behind the Estação do Rossio, this new *ginjinha* bar flaunts a slick, monochrome interior. It's a convivial spot for a *ginjinha* shot served in an edible chocolate cup (€1.65) or a coffee or beer. (Calçada do Carmo 37A; ⏱noon-midnight Sun-Thu, noon-2am Fri & Sat)

Ginjinha Rubi   GINJINHA BAR

24 🍷 Map p46, B1

Squeeze into this hole-in-the-wall bar to natter with locals over a *ginjinha* or three and admire the *azulejos*. (Rua Barros Queirós 27; ⏱7am-midnight)

Bar Rossio   BAR

25 🍷 Map p46, A1

A terrific rooftop spot for an afternoon coffee or drinks as the city lights begin to glow. (Altis Avenida Hotel, Rua 1 Dezembro 120; ⏱7am-1am)

Ginjinha Sem Rival   GINJINHA BAR

26 🍷 Map p46, B1

This old-school, bottle-lined bar is one of the few places that still produces its own *ginjinha* (€1.35 a shot). (Rua Portas de Santo Antão 61; ⏱7am-midnight)

Entertainment

Coliseu dos Recreios   CONCERT HALL

27 ⭐ Map p46, B1

This concert hall stages big-name concerts, theatre, dance and opera. The recent roll-call has included Placebo, Morrissey and Ana Moura. (📞213 240 580; www.coliseulisboa.com; Rua das Portas de Santo Antão 96)

Teatro Nacional de Dona Maria II   THEATRE

28 ⭐ Map p46, B1

Rossio's graceful neoclassical theatre has a somewhat hit-and-miss schedule due to underfunding. Guided tours on Mondays at 11.30am (€6). (📞213 250 800; www.teatro-dmaria.pt; Praça Dom Pedro IV)

Shopping

Loja das Conservas   FOOD

29 🔒 Map p46, A5

What appears to be a gallery is on closer inspection a temple to tinned fish, or *conservas* as the Portuguese say. The retro-wrapped tins are the artworks. They make terrific gifts, and you can try them at the tastings from 4pm to 8pm every Tuesday and Wednesday. (Rua do Arsenal 130; ⏱10am-8pm Mon-Sat, noon-8pm Sun)

Xocoa FOOD

30 Map p46, B3

There's chocolate, chocolate every-where in this truly scrumptious little store, an offshoot of the famous Barcelona brand. Find Lisbon's most delectable chocolate cakes, tortes, truffles and pralines here. Or grab a super-smooth chocolate for a take-away fix. (Rua do Crucifixo 112; ⏱10am-8pm Mon-Sat)

Queijaria Nacional FOOD

31 Map p46, C4

A one-stop cheese shop with varieties from all over Portugal – from pungent and creamy Serra da Estrela to Azores and Alentejo varieties. You can also pair cheese and charcuterie with Por-tuguese wines over a tasting here. (Rua da Conceiçao 8; ⏱10am-8pm)

Understand
What's in a Name?

- - - - - - - - - - - - - - -

Baixa's gridlike streets are named after the trades that once flourish-ed here. Racing you back to those days are roads named after *sapat-eiros* (shoemakers), *correeiros* (saddlers), *douradores* (gilders), *fanqueiros* (cutlers), *ouro* (gold), *prata* (silver) and even *bacalhoeiros* (cod-fishing vessels). Some still reveal traces of their artisanal past; take a stroll to see what's in a name today.

Santos Oficios HANDICRAFTS

32 Map p46, D3

If you have always fancied a hand-embroidered fado shawl, check out this brick-vaulted store. Santos is a must-shop for Portuguese folk art including Madeira lace, blingy Christmas decorations and glazed earthenware. (Rua da Madalena 87; ⏱10am-8pm Mon-Sat)

Discoteca Amália MUSIC

33 Map p46, B2

This shrine to *fadista* Amália Rodri-gues stocks an excellent range of fado and classical CDs. (Rua de Áurea 272; ⏱10am-7pm Mon-Sat)

Napoleão WINE

34 Map p46, C4

This friendly, English-speaking cellar is the go-to place for Portuguese wines and ports, with hundreds of bottles to choose from. Ships worldwide. (Rua dos Fanqueiros 70; ⏱9am-8pm Mon-Sat, 1-8pm Sun)

Rei do Bacalhau GOURMET FOOD

35 Map p46, A5

At this humble 'king of cod' you can buy dried, salted *bacalhau* by the gram. And who can resist those pot-ted cod tongues and fins? Mmmm... (Rua do Arsenal 110; ⏱8am-7.30pm Mon-Sat)

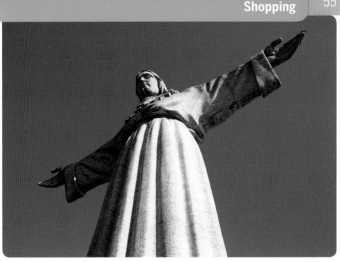

Cristo Rei (Christ King Statue; p50), by artist Francisco Franco de Sousa

Amatudo   CRAFTS

36 🔒 Map p46, D4

This is a one-stop shop for non-kitschy Portuguese gifts like Tricana sardines, beautifully packaged Confi-ança soaps, 3D Belém or tram puzzles, and humorous takes on the Barcelos cockerel. (Rua da Madalena 76; ⏰10.30am-7.30pm Mon-Sat)

Pátio da Galé Lisbon Shop GIFTS

37 🔒 Map p46, B5

Housed in the Pombaline Pátio da Galé (p43) complex, this shop is crammed with 100% Portuguese gifts, ranging from tram tees to cockerel mugs, cork bags to speciality foods. (Rua do Arsenal 15; ⏰9.30am-7.30pm)

Espaço Açores   FOOD

38 🔒 Map p46, C4

The closest you can get to actually visiting the Azores is this attractive shop, where a taste of the islands comes in the form of cheeses, honeys, preserves, passionfruit liqueurs and, apparently, the only tea produced in Europe. (Rua de São Julião 58; ⏰10am-7pm Mon-Fri, 10am-1pm Sat)

Top Sights
Tram 28

Getting There

M Metro Frequent trains (green line) run directly to Martim Moniz, the metro stop closest to tram 28's departure point; Rossio station is a two-minute walk away.

There's a reason why tram 28 tops most travellers' Lisbon wish-list. This rickety, screechy, gloriously old-fashioned ride from Praça Martim Moniz to Campo Ourique is 40 minutes of mood-lifting views and absurdly steep climbs. With its polished wood panelling, bee-yellow paint job and chrome fittings, this century-old tram is like the full-scale model of a fastidious Hornby collector. Use *bom dias* (good mornings) and the powers of persuasion to bag a space by the window and prepare for a self-guided city tour to remember.

Don't Miss

Graça

The grocery stores, wrought-iron lanterns and washing-strewn townhouses seem, at times, close enough to touch as tram 28 scoots along the narrow, curving backstreets of Graça. Keep your eyes out for the graceful twin spires of Igreja de São Vicente de Fora.

Castelo & Alfama

As the tram descends, try to sit on the left side of the carriage for fleeting views across Alfama's mosaic of red rooftops to the Rio Tejo and close-ups of Sé (cathedral). Jump off at Largo das Portas do Sol for an incredible city panorama, or make the short climb up to Castelo de São Jorge. Tram-surfers are often spotted clinging perilously to the doors to dodge paying for a ticket.

Baixa & Chiado

Settle back as you rumble through the Pombaline streets of Baixa and then begin the ascent to the elegant mosaic-tiled Praça Luís de Camões, centred on a statue of its eponymous poet. As the tram climbs higher toward Estrela, there are great snapshot views of the city and river.

Estrela & Prazeres

As tram 28 continues past *azulejo*-lined and pastel-hued facades on the Calçada da Estrela, the neoclassical Palácio da Assembleia da República and the graceful white dome of the neoclassical Basílica da Estrela slide into view. Stay right until the end (Campo Ourique) for a stroll around Cemitério dos Prazeres, built in 1833, dotted with monumental tombs and commanding views down to the river and Ponte 25 de Abril.

☑ Top Tips

▸ You can buy tickets on board or at metro stations.

▸ Want to hop on and off at your leisure? Invest in a 24-hour Carris pass (€6).

▸ Start at Praça Martim Moniz to stand the best chances of getting a seat.

▸ Tram 28 is a pickpockets' playground: watch your valuables.

✗ Take a Break

Hop off halfway at Praça Luís de Camões for coffee at **Café a Brasileira** (Map p28, D5; Rua Garrett 120, Chiado; ⊙8am-2am). All gold swirls and cherubs, this art-deco cafe has been a Lisbon institution since 1905.

Explore

Alfama, Castelo & Graça

This is the Lisbon you have no doubt dreamed about: a Moorish castle slung on a hillside, cobbled alleys twisting to sky-high viewpoints and laundry-strung houses in a fresco painter's palette of colours. In this corner of the city, life is played out on the streets. Fado still rocks as it did way back when, one-pan family bistros fire up their grills at lunchtime, and the neighbourly vibe keeps things alluringly low-key.

The Sights in a Day

☼ Get to **Castelo de São Jorge** (p60) before the crowds do for a peaceful ramble around the Moorish ramparts; tram 28 will drop you nearby. Grab a morning coffee at **Cruzes Credo Café** (p69), then dip into the city's medieval past at **Sé** (cathedral; p66) opposite. Strolling up the hill brings you to Lisbon's best-preserved Roman remains at the **Museu do Teatro Romano** (p67).

☼ A brisk walk uphill brings you to Graça, where you should factor in time to visit the beautifully tiled cloister of **Igreja de São Vicente de Fora** (p66) and jauntily domed **Panteão Nacional** (p66). Wend your way through the mazy backstreets of Alfama, full of neighbourly gossip, flapping laundry and fado music, as the sun begins to set.

☾ Now it's your choice: either cosy up over a romantic courtyard dinner at **Santo António de Alfama** (p68), or head to an intimate fado club like **A Baîuca** (p70) for an evening of gutsy song and good company. Stopping out? Party with the best of them at riverside hot spot **Lux-Frágil** (p70) or linger over a nightcap at rooftop **Memmo Alfama** (p69).

For a local's day in Alfama, see p62.

◉ Top Sights
Castelo de São Jorge (p60)

○ Local LIfe
Alfama Backstreets (p62)

♥ Best of Lisbon

Bars & Nightlife
Memmo Alfama (p69)

Lux-Frágil (p70)

Clube Ferroviário (p69)

Churches, Castles & Palaces
Castelo de São Jorge (p60)

Sé (p66)

Food
Santa Clara dos Cogumelos (p68)

Getting There

🚋 **Tram** Tram 28 bowls through Castelo and Graça. Key stops: Largo das Portas do Sol, Sé and Largo da Graça.

Ⓜ **Metro** The blue line to Santa Apolónia is a quick way of reaching the sights closest to the river.

🚌 **Bus** Take the 734 from Martim Moniz to Santa Apolónia train station for Largo da Graça and Campo de Santa Clara.

Top Sights
Castelo de São Jorge

Gazing grandly over the city, these heavily restored hilltop fortifications evoke Lisbon's history from the bold to the bloody. Settlers first arrived in the area in the 7th century BC, but the castle itself dates to the mid-11th century when the Moors ruled Lisbon and the stronghold was the heart of their *alcáçova* (citadel). Christian crusaders in 1147, royals from the 14th to 16th centuries, and convicts in every century; battles, coronations and an earthquake – this castle has seen it all.

◉ Map p64, B3

ww.castelodesaojorge.pt

adult/child €8.50/5

⊘9am-9pm Mar-Oct, 9am-6pm Nov-Feb

Don't Miss

Ramparts & Garden

Shaded by pine trees, the castle's ramparts afford far-reaching views over Lisbon. From here you can glimpse the river and Ponte 25 de Abril, contrast the gridlike streets of Baixa with the high-rises of the modern districts, and pick out the city's monuments and plazas. Peacocks strut proudly through the adjacent gardens, littered with ruins.

Tower of Ulysses & Periscope

Of all the castle's 11 towers, the Tower of Ulysses has the most gripping history. It once housed the royal treasury and archives and was nicknamed the Torre do Tombo (Tumbling Tower) because the most important things in the kingdom used to 'tumble' into it. It now contains a periscope, or camera obscura, which gives a 360-degree view of the city in real time.

Núcleo Museológico

This museum makes a fair stab at drawing together the different epochs of the castle's history (and prehistory) and spelling them out in artefacts. On display is the fruit of archaeological digs – fragments of Iron Age pottery, Roman wine vessels, medieval oil lamps and coins, 17th-century *azulejos* (hand-painted tiles) and the like.

Archaeological Site

OK, it's time to use your imagination to piece together the parts of the castle's past with a wander around this archaeological site. In a quiet corner of the fortress, you can just about make out where the first settlement was in the 7th century BC, the remains of the mid-11th-century Moorish dwellings and the ruins of the last royal residence, destroyed in the 1755 earthquake.

☑ Top Tips

▶ Join one of the free 1½-hour guided tours of the castle at noon and 4pm daily. Free 20-minute tours of the Tower of Ulysses run half-hourly.

▶ Pick up a free map and guide at the entrance.

▶ Arrive early or late in the day for fewer crowds.

▶ Come back at dusk for perfect snapshots of the illuminated castle.

✗ Take a Break

By day, follow the scent of chargrilled fish to local favourite **Páteo 13** (Map p64, E4; Calçadinha de Santo Estêvão 13; mains €8-12; ⏰11am-11pm Tue-Sun), tucked away on a small, festively decorated plaza in Alfama.

By night, enjoy vertigo-inducing views of Lisbon illuminated, well-prepared cocktails and jazzy beats at nearby **Bar das Imagens** (Map p64, A3; Calçada Marquês de Tancos 1; ⏰11am-11pm Tue-Sun).

Local Life
Alfama Backstreets

Moorish history seeps through the backstreets of this medina-like neighbourhood, an enticing jumble of cobbled alleys filled with flapping laundry and fado song, where *calçadas* (stairways) climb to castle-facing *miradouros* (viewpoints). Alfama and its neighbours, Graça and Castelo, afford snapshots of daily life on flower-draped squares, at weekend flea markets, and in hidden alleys full of unexpected beauty and banter.

1 River Views

Begin your day with views across Alfama's rooftops to the Rio Tejo from the bougainvillea-wreathed **Miradouro de Santa Luzia** (Largo Santa Luzia) on Rua do Limoeiro. At the back, note the blue-and-white *azulejo* tile panels depicting scenes from the Siege of Lisbon in 1147 and Praça do Comércio in the early 18th century.

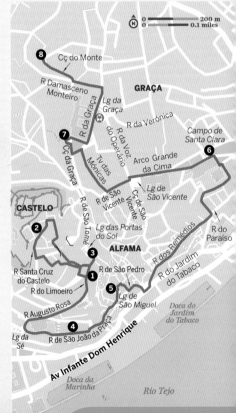

2 Castelo's Side Streets

Every day hundreds flock to Castelo de São Jorge, but few explore the atmospheric web of lanes around the castle, such as **Rua Santa Cruz do Castelo**, studded with pastel-hued houses, hole-in-the-wall bars and grocers. Slow the pace here for a sense of the old Moorish *alcáçova* (citadel), once home to the city's elite.

3 Moorish Gateway

The Moorish gateway **Largo das Portas do Sol** has postcard views of Alfama and Graça. Peer across a mosaic of red rooftops to the Panteão Nacional's ivory-white dome and twin-spired Igreja de São Vicente de Fora.

4 Hidden Azulejos

Following the tram tracks downhill brings you to Sé, Lisbon's fortress-like Gothic cathedral. Behind it is **Rua de São João da Praça**, with vaulted cafes, fado clubs and *azulejo*-clad facades – look out for diamond-tip patterns at No 88 and floral motifs at No 106.

5 Alfama Stroll

At Alfama's higgledy-piggledy heart is **Largo de São Miguel**, identified by its twin-towered chapel and palm tree, and **Rua dos Remédios**, perfect for a mooch with its cafes, grocery stores and galleries. In alleys close by, melancholic fado drifts from open windows, men play backgammon, chefs grill sardines and neighbours trade gossip just as they have for centuries.

6 Flea-Market Finds

To see Graça at its lively best, visit at the weekend when **Campo de Santa Clara** becomes a giant flea market, with locals gathering to sell tat and treasures in the shadow of the gracefully domed Panteão Nacional.

7 Summertime Hang-Out

A much-loved summertime hang-out of Lisboetas is **Miradouro da Graça** (⊙10am-8pm). This terrace, sidling up to the baroque Igreja da Graça, has an incredible vista to the castle sitting plump on the hillside, the river and the Ponte 25 de Abril. Sunset is prime-time viewing at the kiosk terrace. Park yourself at a table under the pine trees for cool drinks and good vibes.

8 Lisbon's Highest Viewpoint

For a top-of-the-city view, huff up to **Miradouro da Senhora do Monte**, one of the lesser-known *miradouros* in Lisbon, despite being the highest. From this pine-shaded plaza, the entire city spreads out picturesquely before you – from the hilltop castle to the Ponte 25 de Abril looping across the river.

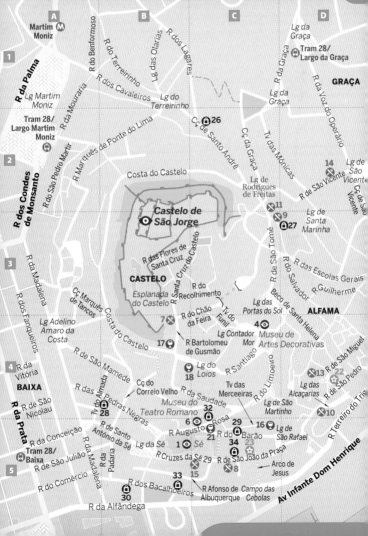

Martim Moniz Ⓜ A

R do Benformoso

R dos Lagares

R das Olarias

Lg da Graça

Tram 28/ Largo da Graça

R da Palma

Lg Martim Moniz

R do Terreirinho

R dos Cavaleiros

R da Mouraria

Lg do Terreirinho

R da Graça

GRAÇA

Tram 28/ Largo Martim Moniz

R dos Condes de Monsanto

R de São Pedro Martir

R Marquês de Ponte do Lima

Cç de Santo André 🔒26

Cç da Graça

Tv das Mónicas

Lg da Graça

R da Voz do Operário

R de São Vicente

14 ✖

Lg de São Vicente

Costa do Castelo

Lg de Rodrigues de Freitas

Cç de São Vicente

🔒11

9 ✖

Lg de Santa Marinha

Castelo de São Jorge ☉

R de São Tomé

🔒27

R da Madalena

R dos Fanqueiros

R das Flores de Santa Cruz

CASTELO

R Santa Cruz Castelo

R do Recolhimento

R das Escolas Gerais

R do Salvador

R Guilherme

Cç Marquês de Tancos

Esplanada do Castelo

Costa do Castelo

7 ✖

R do Chão da Feira

Tv do Funil

Lg das Portas do Sol

Beco de Santa Helena

ALFAMA

Lg Adelino Amaro da Costa

R de São Mamede

17 🔒

R Bartolomeu de Gusmão

Lg Contador Mor

4 ☉ Museu de Artes Decorativas

R da Vitória

BAIXA

R das Almas

18 🔒 Lg do Loios

R Santiago

R de São Miguel

13 ✖ 22 ★

R de São Pedro

R de São Nicolau

Cç do Correio Velho

Tv das Merceeiras

Lg das Alcaçarias

10 ✖

R da Prata

Tv do Almada

28 🔒

Pedras Negras

Museu do Teatro Romano

6 ☉

R de Santo António da Sé

R de São Julião

Lg da Sé

R Augusto Rosa

32 ✖

21 🔒

R do Barão

29 ✖

16 🔒

Lg de São Rafael

Lg de São Martinho

Tv das Merceeiras

R Terreiro do Trigo

Tram 28/ Baixa

1 ☉ **Sé**

34 ✖

23 🔒

R de São João da Praça

R da Conceição

R da Madalena

R da Padaria

R Cruzes da Sé 29

8 ✖

Arco de Jesus

33 🔒

15 ✖

Av Infante Dom Henrique

R do Comércio

R dos Bacalhoeiros

30 🔒

R Afonso de Albuquerque

Campo das Cebolas

R da Alfândega

R da Verónica

E **F** **G** **H**

For reviews see
- ◉ Top Sights — p60
- ◉ Sights — p66
- ✖ Eating — p67
- 🍷 Drinking — p69
- ✪ Entertainment — p70
- 🔒 Shopping — p72

🚇 19

Campo de Santa Clara

🔒 31

Arco Grande da Cima

Campo de Santa Clara

R de Santa Apolónia

Cais de Pedra à Bica do Sapato

🚇 20

Panteão Nacional ◉3

2 ◉
Igreja de São Vicente de Fora

Lg do Outeirinho da Amendoeira

12 ✖

R do Paraíso

Santa Apolónia Train Station

🚇ℹ

Santa Apolónia Ⓜ

R dos Corvos

R do Vigário

R do Museu de Artilharia

✪ 24
25

Calçadinha de Santo Estêvão

R dos Remédios

Av Infante Dom Henrique

Cais de Pedra à Bica do Sapato

R do Jd do Tabaco

Lg do Chafariz de Dentro

◉5
Museu do Fado

Rio Tejo

Doca do Jardim do Tabaco

Ⓝ 0 _____ 400 m
0 _____ 0.2 miles

Sights

Sé

CATHEDRAL

1 ⊙ Map p64, B5

One of Lisbon's icons is the fortress-like Sé, built in 1150 on the site of a mosque soon after Christians recaptured the city from the Moors.

It was sensitively restored in the 1930s. Despite the masses outside, the rib-vaulted interior, lit by a rose window, is calm. Stroll around the cathedral to spy leering gargoyles peeking above the orange trees. (admission free; ⏰9am-7pm Tue-Sat, 9am-5pm Mon & Sun)

Igreja de São Vicente de Fora

CHURCH

2 ⊙ Map p64, E2

Graça's serene, gorgeous Igreja de São Vicente de Fora was founded as a monastery in 1147, revamped by Italian architect Felipe Terzi in the late 16th century, and devastated in the 1755 earthquake. Elaborate blue-and-white *azulejos* dance across almost every wall, echoing the curves of the architecture. On the 1st floor you'll find a one-off collection of panels depicting La Fontaine's moral tales of sly foxes and greedy wolves. Under the marble **sacristy** lie the crusaders' tombs.

Seek out the weeping, cloaked woman holding stony vigil in the eerie **mausoleum**. Have your camera handy for the superb views from the tower. (Largo de São Vicente; adult/child €5/2.50; ⏰10am-6pm Tue-Sun)

Panteão Nacional

MUSEUM

3 ⊙ Map p64, F2

Perched high and mighty above Graça's Campo de Santa Clara, the porcelain-white Panteão Nacional is a baroque beauty. Originally intended as a church, it now pays homage to Portugal's heroes and heroines, including 15th-century explorer Vasco da Gama and *fadista* Amália Rodrigues.

Lavishly adorned with pink marble and gold swirls, its echoing dome resembles an enormous Fabergé egg. Trudge up to the 4th-floor viewpoint for a sunbake and vertigo-inducing views over Alfama and the river. (Campo de Santa Clara; adult/child €4/2; ⏰10am-6pm Tue-Sun)

Museu de Artes Decorativas

MUSEUM

4 ⊙ Map p64, C4

Set in a petite 17th-century palace, the Museu de Artes Decorativas creaks under the weight of treasures including blingy French silverware, priceless Qing vases and Indo-Chinese furniture. It's worth a visit alone to admire the lavish apartments, embellished with baroque *azulejos,* frescos and chandeliers. (Museum of Decorative Arts; www.fress.pt; Largo das Portas do Sol 2; adult/child €4/free; ⏰10am-5pm Wed-Mon)

Museu do Fado

MUSEUM

5 ⊙ Map p64, E4

Fado was born in Alfama. Immerse yourself in its bittersweet symphonies

Understand
José Saramago Foundation

Long closed to the public, the Casa dos Bicos is now the proud new home of the **Fundação José Saramago** (Map p64, B5; www.josesaramago.org; Rua dos Bacalhoeiros 10; adult/child €3/2; ⏲10am-6pm Mon-Sat), which will host exhibitions, readings and conferences and contains the library of the Nobel Prize–winning author. Opposite the Casa dos Bicos stands an olive tree, where Saramago's ashes were scattered in 2011. With its historic resonance and location close to the river, there could not be a more fitting tribute than this 16th-century landmark for the country's literary heavyweight. Known for his discursive, cynical and darkly humorous novels, Saramago gained worldwide attention after winning the Nobel Prize in 1998. His best works mine the depth of the human experience and are often set in a uniquely Portuguese landscape.

at the Museu do Fado. This engaging museum traces fado's history from its working-class roots to international stardom.

The collection takes in discs, recordings, posters, a hall of fame and a recreated guitar workshop. Afterwards, pick up some fado of your own at the shop. (www.museudofado.pt; Largo do Chafariz de Dentro; admission €5; ⏲10am-6pm Tue-Sun)

Museu do Teatro Romano MUSEUM

6 ◉ Map p64, C5

The ultramodern Museu do Teatro Romano catapults you back to Emperor Augustus' rule in Olisipo (Lisbon). Upstairs is the star attraction – a ruined **Roman theatre** extended in AD 57, buried in the 1755 earthquake and finally unearthed in 1964. The museum was closed for renovation work at the time of writing and is set to reopen in 2015. (Roman Theatre Museum; www.museuteatroromano.pt; Pátio do Aljube 5; admission free; ⏲10am-1pm & 2-6pm Tue-Sun)

Eating

Claras em Castelo PORTUGUESE €

7 🍴 Map p64, B4

Just steps from the castle, this tiny restaurant enjoys a loyal following for its warm service and solid home cooking. Dishes like *bacalhau com natas* (cod in a creamy sauce) pair nicely with reasonably priced wines. Booking ahead is highly advisable. (☎218 853 071; Rua Bartolomeu de Gusmão 31; mains €8-11; ⏲Thu-Tue)

Pois Café

CAFE €

8 🍴 Map p64, C5

Boasting a laid-back vibe, Pois Café has creative salads, sandwiches and fresh juices, plus a delicious daily special (soup and main for €9.50). Its sofas invite lazy afternoons spent reading novels and sipping coffee. (www.poiscafe.com; Rua de São João da Praça 93; mains €7-10; ⏰1-11pm Mon, 11am-11pm Tue-Sun; 🛜)

Marcelino Pão e Vinho

PORTUGUESE €

9 🍴 Map p64, C3

This narrow cafe has just three tables inside and two outside. What it lacks in space, however, it makes up for in atmosphere, with local artworks on the walls, occasional live music, refreshing sangria, and salads, sandwiches, quiches, desserts and other light bites. (📞916 946 213; Rua do Salvador 62; snacks €2-5; ⏰9am-11pm Thu-Tue; 🛜)

Medrosa d'Alfama

CAFE €

10 🍴 Map p64, D4

This friendly new cafe has a handful of tables on one of Alfama's prettiest squares. It's a fine spot for a beer with grilled *chorizo*, toasties (try the goat cheese with walnuts and honey), or coffee and cake. (Largo de São Rafael 6; ⏰2pm-midnight Thu-Mon, 5pm-midnight Wed)

Princesa do Castelo

CAFE €

11 🍴 Map p64, C2

This bright and chirpy vegetarian cafe positively radiates good health with vegetarian, vegan and macrobiotic dishes that play up the wild and the organic. Besides lunch specials like veggie moussaka and tofu curry, it's a nice place to stop for a juice, smoothie or Ayurvedic tea. (📞961 156 792; Rua do Salvador 64A; snacks €3-5, lunch specials €7-8.50; ⏰10am-midnight Tue-Sun; 🍴)

Santa Clara dos Cogumelos

INTERNATIONAL €€

12 🍴 Map p64, F2

If you're a mushroom fan, this novel restaurant in the old market hall on Campo de Santa Clara is simply magic. The menu is an ode to the humble *cogumelo* (mushroom). Go for *petiscos* (tapas) like organic shitake with garlic and coriander, mains like risotto with porcini and black trumpets, and perhaps mushroom ice cream with brownies for dessert. (📞218 870 661; www.santaclaradoscogumelos.com; Campo de Santa Clara 7; petiscos €5-8, mains €14-18; ⏰7.30-11pm Tue-Fri, 12.30-3.30pm & 7.30-11pm Sat; 🍴)

Santo António de Alfama

PORTUGUESE €€

13 🍴 Map p64, D4

This bistro wins the award for Lisbon's loveliest courtyard: all vines, twittering budgies and fluttering laundry. The interior is a silver-screen shrine, while the menu stars tasty *petiscos*: Gorgonzola-stuffed mushrooms, roasted aubergines with yoghurt, as well as more filling traditional Portuguese dishes. (📞218 881 328; www.siteantonio.com; Beco de São Miguel 7; mains €13.50-21; ⏱noon-2am)

Bistro Gato Pardo INTERNATIONAL €€

14 🍴 Map p64, D2

One of Lisbon's coolest cats, Gato Pardo is a wonderfully chilled cafe, with a mishmash of vintage furniture, splashes of art on the wall and good vibes. The salads, pasta dishes and fish mains are winningly fresh. (📞934 889 027; Rua de São Vicente 10; mains €7-18; ⏱11am-10pm Fri-Tue)

Cruzes Credo Café CAFE €€

15 🍴 Map p64, C5

In the shadow of the grand cathedral, this youthful, jazz-loving cafe has earned a local following for its cosy ambience and eclectic menu. Stop in for coffees, drinks, salads, sandwiches, crêpes, burgers, and decadent chocolate cake. (Rua Cruzes da Sé 29; mains €7-12; ⏱10am-2am)

Drinking

Memmo Alfama BAR

16 🍺 Map p64, C5

Wow, what a view! Alfama unfolds like origami from the stylishly decked roof terrace of the Memmo Alfama hotel. It's perfect sundowner material, with dreamy views over the rooftops and spires down to the Rio Tejo. (www.memmoalfama.com; Travessa das Merceeiras 27; ⏱6-11pm)

Wine Bar do Castelo WINE BAR

17 🍺 Map p64, B4

Located near the entrance to the Castelo São Jorge, this laid-back wine bar serves more than 150 Portuguese wines by the glass, along with gourmet smoked meats, cheeses, olives and other tasty accompaniments. Nuno, the multilingual owner, is a welcoming host and a fount of knowledge about all things wine-related. (Rua Bartolomeu de Gusmão 13; ⏱noon-10pm)

Chapitô BAR

18 🍺 Map p64, B4

This alternative theatre, with a circus school attached, offers fantastic views from its bar and is a top choice for a sundowner or a late-night drink overlooking the city. (Costa do Castelo 7; ⏱noon-2am)

Clube Ferroviário CLUB

19 🍺 Map p64, H1

Above Santa Apolónia train station, this former social club of Lisbon's railworkers has been transformed into an intriguing nightspot with DJs and occasional concerts; the best feature is the roof terrace with Tejo views. (Rua de Santa Apolónia 59; ⏱4pm-2am Tue-Thu, 6pm-4am Fri & Sat, 4pm-midnight Sun)

Lux-Frágil
CLUB

20 Map p64, H2

Lisbon's ice-cool, must-see club, Lux hosts big-name DJs spinning electro and house. It's run by ex-Frágil maestro Marcel Reis and part-owned by John Malkovich. Grab a spot on the terrace to see the sun rise over the Tejo.

Style policing is heartwarmingly lax but arrive after 4am at weekends and you might have trouble getting in because of the crowds. (www.luxfragil. com; Avenida Infante Dom Henrique, Santo Apolónia; ⊙11pm-6am Thu-Sat)

Café Pit
CAFE

21 Map p64, C5

If you're craving a caffeine hit before the climb up to the castle, this is the perfect pit stop. It's also a mellow spot for tapas, light bites (€3 to €15) and wine. (Rua Augusto Rosa 19-21; ⊙8am-11pm)

Entertainment

A Baîuca
FADO

22 Map p64, D4

On a good night, walking into A Baîuca is like gate crashing a family party. It's a special place with *fado vadio*, where locals take a turn and spectators hiss if anyone dares to chat during the singing. There's a €25 minimum spend and the food stops around 10pm, though the fado goes on until midnight. Reserve ahead. (☑218 867 284; Rua de São Miguel 20; ⊙8pm-midnight Thu-Mon)

Clube de Fado
FADO

23 Map p64, C5

Clube de Fado hosts the cream of the fado crop in vaulted, dimly lit surrounds. Big-name *fadistas* performing here include Joana Amendoeira and Miguel Capucho, alongside celebrated guitarists such as José Fontes Rocha. The food is less outstanding, so come for drinks and perhaps appetisers. (☑218 852 704; www.clube-de-fado.com; Rua de São João da Praça 92; ⊙8pm-2am)

Senhor Fado
FADO

24 Map p64, F3

Small and lantern-lit, this is a cosy spot for *fado vadio*. *Fadista* Ana Marina and guitarist Duarte Santos make a great double act. (☑218 874 298; www.sr-fado.com; Rua dos Remédios 176; ⊙8pm-2am Wed-Sat)

Mesa de Frades
FADO

25 Map p64, E3

A magical place to hear fado, tiny Mesa de Frades used to be a chapel.

☑ Top Tip

Cover Charge

Most fado places have a minimum cover charge of €15 to €25, though a fixed menu can cost anything up to €50. The quality of food can be hit and miss; if in doubt, it might be worth asking if you can just order a bottle of wine.

Understand

Fado

There is no better way to tune into the Portuguese psyche, some say, than by listening to fado: plaintive, bittersweet music overflowing with emotional intensity. Ask locals what fado means and you'll get a different answer every time. And indeed, the more you listen to it, the more you realise how diverse the genre is. As one *fadista* (singer of fado) sagely put it: 'Fado is life itself: happiness, sadness, poetry, history.'

The Origins of Fado

Fado's origins are largely traceable to the backstreets of working-class Alfama. The ditties of homesick sailors, the poetic ballads of the Moors, the bluesy songs of Brazilian slaves – all are cited as possible influences, and no doubt fado is a blend of these and more. Central to all forms of fado is *saudade,* a hard-to-translate, distinctly Portuguese concept redolent of nostalgic longing. This often underpins recurring themes in fado such as destiny (fado means 'fate'), remorse, heartbreak and loneliness. In Lisbon, fado typically consists of a solo vocalist singing to the accompaniment of a 12-stringed Portuguese guitar and viola.

Famous Fadistas

If fado was born in Alfama, it was Amália Rodrigues (1920–99) who took it to the world with her heartbreaking trills and poetic soul. The so-called Rainha do Fado (Queen of Fado) still holds a special place in the hearts of the Portuguese. More recently, *fadistas* have continued to broaden fado's scope and appeal – often adding a pinch of blues, a splash of Argentine tango or a dash of flamenco. The best known of the new generation *fadistas* is Mariza, whose 2007 *Concerto em Lisboa* and 2008 *Terra* albums received Latin Grammy nominations.

Fado in Alfama

Wander through Alfama today and you'll almost certainly hear the strains of fado drifting from open windows of dimly lit clubs. Performances range from light-hearted *fado vadio,* a kind of jam session where amateurs take turns to sing, to fully blown professional acts. Which you prefer is a matter of taste. Wherever you go, when the lights go down, the audience falls silent – a sign of respect for the song of the soul.

It's tiled with exquisite *azulejos* and has just a handful of tables. The show begins around 11pm. Skip the food and stick to drinks. (☎917 029 436; Rua dos Remédios 139A; ⊙7pm-2am Mon-Sat)

Shopping

Cortiço & Netos   HOMEWARES

26 🔒 Map p64, C2

A wonder wall of fabulous *azulejos* greets you as you enter this very special space. It's the vision of brothers Pedro, João, Ricardo and Tiago Cortiço, whose grandfather dedicated more than 30 years to gathering, storing and selling discontinued Portuguese industrial tiles. Reviving the family trade, they are experts on the *azulejo*. (www.corticoenetos.com; Calçada de Santo André 66; ⊙10am-1pm & 2-7pm Mon-Sat)

Garbags   BAGS

27 🔒 Map p64, D3

This ecofriendly outfit sells messenger bags, iPhone cases, wallets, handbags and zipper pouches cleverly made from former coffee sacks, potato chip bags, juice containers and other recycled materials. The gear seems durable (and waterproof) and the look is somewhat sleek, if you don't mind the corporate logos. (www.garbags.eu; Rua do Salvador 56; ⊙10am-8pm Mon-Sat, 10am-6pm Sun)

Zazou   HANDICRAFTS

28 🔒 Map p64, B4

Zazou is a craft store, cafe and deli rolled lovingly into one. Browse for

gifts like Alentejo ceramics, wicker baskets and donkey-milk soap (works wonders on the complexion, apparently), before comparing purchases over a plate of Portuguese cheese and charcuterie. (Calçada do Correio Velho 7; ⊙10am-7pm)

O Voo da Andorinha   GIFTS

29 🔒 Map p64, C5

Candy-bright beads, hand-stitched swallows, embroidered accessories and quirky furnishings made with recycled junk – you'll find all of this and more at this adorable boutique near the cathedral. (Rua do Barão 22; ⊙10.30am-7.30pm Tue-Sat)

Silva & Feijó   FOOD

30 🔒 Map p64, B5

Planning a picnic? Stop by this beamed store for sheep's cheese from the Seia mountains, sardine pâté, rye bread, *salsichas* (sausages) and other Portuguese goodies. (Rua dos Bacalhoeiros 117; ⊙10am-7pm Mon-Sat)

Feira da Ladra   MARKET

31 🔒 Map p64, F2

Browse for back-of-the-lorry treasures at this massive flea market. You'll find old records, coins, baggy pants, dog-eared poetry books and other attic junk. Haggle hard and watch your wallet – it isn't called 'thieves market' for nothing. (Campo de Santa Clara; ⊙7am-5pm Tue & Sat)

Feira da Ladra

Arte da Terra
GIFTS

32 🔒 Map p64, C4

In the stables of a centuries-old bishop's palace, Arte da Terra brims with authentic Portuguese crafts including Castello Branco embroideries, nativity figurines, handpainted *azulejos*, fado CDs and quality goods (umbrellas, aprons, writing journals) made from cork. (Rua Augusto Rosa 40; ☺11am-8pm)

Loja dos Descobrimentos
HANDICRAFTS

33 🔒 Map p64, B5

Watch artisans carefully painting handmade *azulejos* at this workshop and store near the Casa dos Bicos. Fruits and flowers, boats, culinary motifs or geometric – tiles are available in myriad colours and designs. (www.loja-descobrimentos.com; Rua dos Bacalhoeiros 14A; ☺9am-7pm)

Garrafeira da Sé
WINE

34 🔒 Map p64, C5

Inebriating Lisboetas since 1927, this vaulted cellar behind Sé stocks 600 Portuguese wines and vintage ports. Try them first at the tasting tables. (Rua de São João da Praça; ☺9am-7pm Mon-Fri, 9am-6pm Sat)

Top Sights
Museu Nacional do Azulejo

Getting There

The museum is 3km north of Graça and Santa Apolónia station.

🚌 **Bus** The 759 and 794, coming from central Lisbon, both stop at Praça do Comércio and Santa Apolónia.

When Queen Dona Leonor founded the Convento do Madre de Deus in 1509, she surely had no idea that the Manueline convent would one day become a stunning tribute to the *azulejo* (hand-painted tile). Well worth a detour, this exceptional museum unravels 500 years of Portuguese history and craftsmanship. A day on the tiles here takes you through chapels with evocative religious panels, corridors emblazoned with Renaissance hunting scenes and rooms dancing with geometric detail.

Azulejos (hand-painted tiles) at Museu Nacional do Azulejo

Don't Miss

Sala de Grande Vista de Lisboa

Tucked away on the 2nd floor, the early 18th-century Great View of Lisbon is the museum's undisputed highlight. Attributed to Spanish tile painter Gabriel del Barco, the huge panoramic panel beautifully encapsulates the city before the earthquake struck in 1755. Pick out Lisbon's seven hills, riverfront and landmarks past and present in the intricately painted blue and white *azulejos*.

Nossa Senhora da Vida

Made up of 1498 tiles, the late 16th-century Altarpiece of Our Lady of Life is one of Portugal's earliest *azulejo* masterpieces. *Trompe l'œil* diamond-tip tiles fringe the base, while ivy-clad columns frame erudite evangelists St John and St Luke, and the centrepiece scene showing the Adoration of the Shepherds.

Church

This Mannerist church in high baroque style is a breathtakingly lavish gilt, fresco and *azulejo* confection. Cherubs appear to flutter above the gilded altarpieces and the ceiling is festooned with frescos depicting the life of the Virgin and Christ. Look for late 17th-century Dutch tile panels showing Moses and the Burning Bush, Franciscans at prayer and the Cortege of Shepherds.

Capela de Santo António

On the 1st floor, this chapel is a shrine to Franciscan preacher St Anthony of Lisbon. Commissioned by King João V, it's a stellar example of Portuguese baroque, with parquetry flooring, intricate wood carvings and a prized 18th-century terracotta crib. The blue-and-white *azulejo* panels show scenes from the life of hermit saints and the miracles of St Anthony.

---

www.museudoazulejo.pt

Rua Madre de Deus 4

adult/child €5/2.50, 1st Sun of the month free

🕑10am-6pm Tue-Sun

☑ Top Tips

▶ If you're on a budget, visit on Sunday when entry is free until 2pm.

▶ The permanent collection is huge – allow two to three hours to do the museum justice.

✖ Take a Break

Lodged in the former refectory, the museum **cafe** (snacks & mains €5–9) is smothered in 19th-century culinary *azulejos* (hand-painted tiles) – rabbits, chickens, fish and the like. It opens onto a leafy courtyard and is an atmospheric place for a coffee and crêpe or a lunch special.

Explore

Belém

In Belém, Atlantic breezes, grandiose nautical monuments and boats gliding along the wide Rio Tejo cast you back to those pioneering days of the Age of Discovery, when the world was Portugal's colonial oyster. And at dusk, when the crowds subside and the softening light paints the monastery's Manueline turrets gold, this riverside neighbourhood is yours alone for exploring.

MIGUEL SANZ/GETTY IMAGES ©

The Sights in a Day

☼ Rise early and make straight for Belém's blockbuster sight, the sublime **Mosteiro dos Jerónimos** (p78), to have the Manueline church and cloister (almost) to yourself. Next up, take a right royal stroll around the **Museu Nacional dos Coches** (p83), a little girl's dream of fairy-tale carriages.

☼ For lunch, go alfresco at one of the park-facing bistros on Rua Vieira Portuense. Your afternoon begins artily with Warhol, Picasso, Miró et al at the contemporary **Museu Colecção Berardo** (p80). Spend the rest of the afternoon rolling with the waves of Portugal's grand maritime past (p126), including exploring the Age of Discovery icon **Torre de Belém** (pictured left; p83).

★ Catch a classic sunset over the Rio Tejo, sipping drinks on the laid-back terrace of **Bar 38° 41'** (p87) at the Doca do Bom Sucesso. Wind down your day with imaginative cuisine at the Michelin-starred, river-facing **Feitoria** (p86), or wine and Portuguese classics at the intimate **Enoteca de Belém** (p86).

👁 Top Sights

Mosteiro dos Jerónimos (p78)

Museu Colecção Berardo (p80)

🖤 Best of Lisbon

Azulejos
Mosteiro dos Jerónimos (p78)

Churches, Castles & Palaces
Igreja Santa Maria de Belém (p79)

Contemporary Art & Design
Museu Colecção Berardo (p80)

For Kids
Museu de Marinha (p83)

Pastelarias & Cafes
Antiga Confeitaria de Belém (p85)

Getting There

🚋 **Tram** The easiest, quickest and most scenic way to reach Belém from downtown Lisbon. 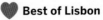Tram 15 runs from Praça da Figueira to Belém via Alcântara (around a 30-minute journey). Tram 18 runs from Cais do Sodré to Ajuda.

🚌 **Bus** Bus 28 operates frequently (several hourly) between Belém and central Lisbon, stopping in Praça do Comércio and Cais do Sodré.

Top Sights
Mosteiro dos Jerónimos

Diogo de Boitaca's creative vision and King Manuel I's gold-laden coffers gave rise to this fantasy fairy tale of a monastery, founded in 1501 to trumpet Vasco da Gama's discovery of a sea route to India. Now a Unesco World Heritage Site, Jerónimos was once populated by monks of the Order of St Jerome, whose spiritual job for four centuries was to comfort sailors and pray for the king's soul. When the order was dissolved in 1833, the monastery was used as a school and orphanage until about 1940.

👁 Map p82, C2

www.mosteirojeroni-mos.pt

Praça do Império

adult/child €10/5

🕙10am-6.30pm Tue-Sun, free 10am-2pm Sun

Don't Miss

Igreja Santa Maria de Belém
Entering the church through the western portal, you'll notice tree-trunk-like columns growing into the ceiling, itself a spiderweb of stone. Navigator Vasco da Gama is interred in the lower chancel, left of the entrance, opposite 16th-century poet Luís Vaz de Camões. From the upper choir is a superb view of the church; the rows of seats are Portugal's first Renaissance woodcarvings.

Cloister
The honey-stone Manueline cloister drips with organic detail in its delicately scalloped arches, twisting auger-shell turrets and columns intertwined with leaves, vines and knots. Pick out symbols of the age, like the armillary sphere and the cross of the Military Order, plus gargoyles and fantastical beasties on the upper level.

Chapter House & Refectory
Vines, flowers, cherubs and reliefs of St Jerome and St Bernard frame the Chapter House's 16th-century portal holding the tomb of Portuguese historian Alexandre Herculano. In the vaulted refectory, 18th-century *azulejo* (hand-painted tile) panels depict the miracle of the loaves and fishes and scenes from the life of Joseph. António Campelo's evocative mural shows the Adoration of the Shepherds.

South Portal
A riot of pinnacles and lacy stonework, the South Portal is the elaborate handiwork of 16th-century architect João de Castilho. The figure of Nossa Senhora de Belém (Our Lady of Bethlehem) sits surrounded by apostles, prophets and angels. Note Henry the Navigator, high on a pedestal, and the tympanum above the door, revealing scenes from the life of St Jerome.

DMITRY SHAKIN/GETTY IMAGES ©

☑ Top Tips

▶ Arrive early or late to appreciate the monastery at its serene best.

▶ Bone up on the monastery's history in the timeline room on the upper level of the cloister.

▶ Visit on Sunday when entry is free until 2pm.

✕ Take a Break

Just a couple of steps away is the Antiga Confeitaria de Belém (p85), serving Lisbon's best custard tarts, with a slice of nostalgia.

An appealing lunch spot is **Alecrim & Manjerona** (Map p82, D2; ☎ 213 620 642; Rua Embaixador 143; light meals & lunches €3-8; ☺10am-7pm Tue-Sat), a sweet grocery store, cafe, deli and wine bar. Besides delicious homemade cakes and tarts, it rustles up wallet-friendly daily specials.

Top Sights
Museu Colecção Berardo

What do you mean you've never heard of it? Bankrolled by Portugal's biggest art collector and billionaire José Berardo, this gallery can hold its own with the Tates and Guggenheims of this world. Yet, incredibly, it is still off the must-see sightseeing radar. Dadaism, minimalism, kinetic art, surrealism and conceptualism; works by Picasso, Dubuffet, Warhol, Yves Klein, Pollock, Miró and Lichtenstein – this mind-blowing collection spans the entire spectrum of modern and contemporary art, from 1960 to 2010. Go. Go today.

👁 Map p82, B3

www.museuberardo.pt

Praça do Império

admission free

🕙10am-7pm Tue-Sun

Museu Colecção Berardo

Don't Miss

British & American Pop Art

Race back to the 1950s and '60s contemplating pop-art masterpieces from both sides of the pond. Warhol's silk-screened portrait of Judy Garland, *Ten Foot Flowers*, *Brillo Box* tower and *Campbell's Soup* steal the limelight. Look too for David Hockney's *Picture Emphasising Stillness* and Lichtenstein's *Interior with Restful Painting*.

Cubism & Dadaism

Several abstract pieces by Picasso, daddy of cubism, are on display, among them his early 20th-century *Tête de Femme* and *Femme dans un Fauteuil*. The anti-war Dadaists also sought to break with conventional art forms. Emblematic of the movement is French artist Marcel Duchamp's 1914 *Le Porte Bouteilles* (Bottle Dryer).

Surrealism

Explore outlandish works by Man Ray, such as his mixed-media *Café Man Ray* and *Talking Picture*, and other standouts of the movement such as Magritte's spacey *Le Gouffre Argenté,* Joan Miró's *Figure à la Bougie,* Max Ernst's inky *Paysage Noir* and Jean Arp's teardrop-like *Feuilles Placées Selon les Lois du Hasard*. For a different perspective, zoom in on the monochromatic photography of Lisbon-born Fernando Lemos.

Modern & Contemporary Sculpture

Sculptures stopping you in your tracks by the entrance include Niki de Saint-Phalle's curvaceous, rainbow-bright *Les Baigneuses* (Swimmers), Pedro Cabrita Reis' industrial-meets-abstract *Amarração*, and Joana Vasconcelos' green wine-bottle wonder, *Nectar*. Inside, look for bronze creations by Antony Gormley, Barry Flanagan and Henry Moore.

STOCKPHOTOSART/SHUTTERSTOCK ©

☑ Top Tips

▶ Pick up a free guide at the entrance for some background on the permanent exhibition.

▶ Visit the website for details of upcoming temporary exhibitions; these are held on level 0.

▶ Allow at least a couple of hours to do this gallery justice.

✗ Take a Break

Join the snaking queue for Belém's tastiest falafel (both hands required), sardine baguettes and Mexican salads at nearby **Pão Pão Queijo Queijo** (Map p82, C2; ☏ 213 626 369; Rua de Belém 124; sandwiches €4; ☀8am-midnight Mon-Sat, 8am-8pm Sun; ✗).

One of Lisbon's iconic vintage trams has been born again as the nicely chilled **Banana Cafe** (Map p82, C2; Largo dos Jerónimos; ☀10am-2am), with tables set up under the trees. It's a relaxed spot for a coffee, smoothie or light snack.

For reviews see
- ◉ Top Sights   p78
- ◉ Sights   p83
- ✕ Eating   p85
- ◌ Drinking   p87
- ✪ Entertainment   p87
- ⊞ Shopping   p87

AJUDA

Tv da Memória

R General João Almeida

Cç da Ajuda

Cç do Galvão

Jardim do Ultramar

Jardim Botânico Tropical

Tv do Marta Pinto

Museu Nacional dos Coches

R do Embaixador

R da Junqueira

R dos Jerónimos

Mosteiro dos Jerónimos

Lg dos Jerónimos

R de Belém

R Vieira Portuense

Pç Afonso de Albuquerque

Av da Índia

Belém Train Station

BELÉM

Museu Nacional de Arqueologia

Museu de Marinha

Pç do Império

Museu Colecção Berardo

Doca de Belém

Padrão dos Descobrimentos

Rio Tejo

R Dom Lourenço de Almeida

R Dom Francisco de Almeida

Av do Restelo

Av de Brasília

R Bartolomeu Dias

Av da Índia

Doca do Bom-Sucesso

Torre de Belém

500 m
0.25 miles

Sights

Torre de Belém   TOWER

1 ◎ Map p82, A4

Jutting out onto the Rio Tejo, this World Heritage–listed fortress epitomises the Age of Discovery. Breathe in to climb a narrow spiral staircase to the tower, affording sublime views over Belém and the river.

Francisco de Arruda designed the pearly-grey chess piece in 1515 to defend Lisbon's harbour, and nowhere else is the lure of the Atlantic more powerful. The Manueline show-off flaunts filigree stonework, meringue-like cupolas and – just below the western tower – a stone rhinoceros. (www.torrebelem.pt; adult/child €6/3, 1st Sun of the month free; ◎10am-6.30pm Tues-Sun)

Padrão dos Descobrimentos   MUSEUM

2 ◎ Map p82, C3

Like a caravel frozen in mid-swell, the monolithic Padrão dos Descobrimentos was inaugurated in 1960 on the 500th anniversary of Henry the Navigator's death. The 52m-high limestone giant is chock-full of Portuguese bigwigs. At the prow is Henry, while behind him are explorers Vasco da Gama, Diogo Cão, Fernão de Magalhães and 29 other greats.

Do take the lift (or puff up 267 steps) to the windswept *miradouro* (viewpoint) for 360-degree views over the river. The mosaic in front of the monument charts the routes of Portu-guese mariners. (Discoveries Monument; www.padraodosdescobrimentos.pt; Avenida de Brasília; adult/child €3/2; ◎10am-7pm, closed Mon in low season)

Museu Nacional dos Coches   MUSEUM

3 ◎ Map p82, D2

Cinderella wannabes feel right at home at the palatial Museu Nacional dos Coches, which dazzles with its world-class collection of 17th- to 19th-century coaches. The stuccoed, frescoed halls of the former royal riding stables display gold coaches so heavy and ornate, it's a wonder they could move at all. Stunners include Pope Clement XI's scarlet-and-gold *Coach of the Oceans*. (National Coach Museum; en.museudoscoches.pt; Praça Afonso de Albuquerque; adult/child €6/3, 1st Sun of the month free; ◎10am-6pm Tue-Sun)

Museu de Marinha   MUSEUM

4 ◎ Map p82, B3

The Museu de Marinha is a nautical flashback to the Age of Discovery with

☑️ Top Tip

Sunday Saver

Want to save on sightseeing? Visit Belém on a Sunday when the big-hitter sights, including the Mosteiro dos Jerónimos, Torre de Belém, Museu de Marinha, Museu Nacional de Arqueologia and Museu Nacional dos Coches, offer free entry from 10am to 2pm.

Understand

The Age of Discovery

The 15th and 16th centuries were Portugal's golden age, when the small kingdom built itself into a massive imperial power and Europe's wealthiest monarchy. Dom João set the ball rolling when he conquered Ceuta, Morocco, in 1415. It was a turning point in Portuguese history.

Manueline Riches

Portugal's biggest breakthrough came in 1497 during the reign of Manuel I, when Vasco da Gama reached southern India. With African gold and slaves and spices from the East, Portugal was soon rolling in riches. Manuel I was so thrilled by the discoveries that he ordered a frenzied building spree in celebration of the age. Top of his list was the Mosteiro dos Jerónimos in Belém, later to become his pantheon.

Enter Spain

Spain had also jumped on the exploration bandwagon and was soon disputing Portuguese claims. Christopher Columbus' 1492 'discovery' of America led to a fresh outburst of jealous conflict. It was resolved by the pope in the 1494 Treaty of Tordesillas, which divided the world between the two great powers along a line 370 leagues west of Cape Verde.

Epic Voyage

The rivalry spurred the first circumnavigation of the world. In 1519 Portuguese navigator Fernão de Magalhães (Ferdinand Magellan), his allegiance transferred to Spain after a tiff with Manuel I, set off to prove the Spice Islands (Moluccas) lay in Spanish 'territory'. He perished in the Philippines in 1521 but one of his ships reached the islands and then sailed home via the Cape of Good Hope, proving the earth was round.

Sinking Ship

By the 1570s, the huge cost of expeditions and an empire was taking its toll. Sebastião's mortal defeat at the 1578 Battle of Alcácer-Quibir launched a downward spiral. When his successor, Cardinal Henrique, died in 1580, Felipe II of Spain fought for and won the throne. This marked the end of centuries of independence and Portugal's glorious moment on the world stage.

its armadas of model ships, cannonballs and shipwreck booty. Dig for buried treasure like Vasco da Gama's portable wooden altar, 17th-century globes (note Australia's absence) and the polished private quarters of UK-built royal yacht *Amélia*. A separate building houses royal barges, 19th-century fire-fighting machines and seaplanes. (Naval Museum; Praça do Império; adult/child €6/3, 1st Sun of the month free; ☺10am-6pm Tue-Sun)

Museu Nacional de Arqueologia   MUSEUM

5 ◉ Map p82, C2

Housed in the Mosteiro dos Jerónimos' western wing, this intriguing stash contains Mesolithic flintstones, Egyptian mummies inside elaborately painted sarcophagi and beautifully wrought Bronze Age jewellery. Even more curious is the collection of statues dedicated to Roman deities. (National Archaeology Museum; www.museuarqueologia.pt; Praça do Império; adult/child €5/free, 1st Sun of the month free; ☺10am-6pm Tue-Sun)

Jardim Botânico Tropical   GARDENS

6 ◉ Map p82, C2

Far from the madding crowd, these botanical gardens bristle with hundreds of tropical species from date palms to monkey puzzle trees. Spread across 7 hectares, it's a peaceful, shady retreat on a sweltering summer's day. A highlight is the Macau garden complete with mini pagoda, where bamboo rustles and a cool stream

trickles. Tots love to clamber over the gnarled roots of a banyan tree and spot the waddling ducks and geese. (www2. iict.pt; Calçada do Galvão; adult/child €2/1; ☺10am-8pm May-Aug, shorter hours in winter)

Eating

Antiga Confeitaria de Belém   PATISSERIE €

7 🍴 Map p82, C2

Since 1837 this patisserie has been transporting locals to sugar-coated nirvana with heavenly *pastéis de Belém*, the crisp pastry nests filled with custard cream, baked at 200°C for that perfect golden crust, then lightly dusted with cinnamon. Admire *azulejos* in the vaulted rooms or devour a

---

Understand
Pastéis de Belém

The origins of heavenly *pastéis de Belém* (aka *pastéis de nata*) stretch back to an early 19th-century sugarcane refinery next to the Mosteiro dos Jerónimos. The liberal revolution swept through Portugal in 1820 and by 1834 all monasteries had been shut down, the monks expelled. Desperate to survive, some clerics saw the light in all that sugar and *pastéis de Belém* were born. The top-secret custard tart recipe hasn't changed since then and shall forever serve as a reminder that calories need not be sinful. Amen.

still-warm tart at the counter and try to guess the secret ingredient. (Rua de Belém 86-88; pastries €1-2.50; ⏰8am-11pm)

Enoteca de Belém
PORTUGUESE, WINE BAR €€

8 Map p82, D2

Tucked down a quiet lane just off Belém's main thoroughfare, this wine bar serves tasty Portuguese classics (try the octopus or the grilled Iberian pork), matched by an excellent selection of full-bodied Douro reds and refreshing Alentejan whites. The atmosphere is a mix of elegance (artwork, bottle-lined walls) and casual. (📞213 631 511; Travessa do Marta Pinto 10; mains €12-17 ; ⏰1-11pm Tue-Sun)

Pastéis de Belém (aka pastéis de nata)

MATTHEW HANCOCK/GETTY IMAGES ©

Espaço Espelho d'Água
FUSION €€

9 Map p82, C4

Part gallery, part restaurant, part cultural space, the new Espaço Espelho d'Água wings you back to the Age of Discovery with its worldly menu and Padrão dos Descobrimentos views from its riverside terrace. On the menu: Portuguese dishes with a pinch of colonial sugar and spice, from cassava soup with clams to cod ceviche with sweet potato and coconut. (📞213 010 510; Avenida de Brasília, Espelho d'Água; light mains €9-13.50; ⏰10am-midnight)

2 a 8
PORTUGUESE €€

10 Map p82, D2

The welcome is warm at this slickly modern bistro, which pairs spot-on Portuguese food with a well-edited wine list. The *petiscos* (tapas) and mains like Setúbal cuttlefish with razor clam rice and duck breast with celery purée, asparagus and orange are big on flavour and nicely presented. Save room for the winningly smooth chocolate mousse. (📞213 639 055; www.restaurantebelem2a8.com; Rua de Belém 2; mains €11-17, 3-course business lunch €16; ⏰noon-10.30pm Tue-Sun)

Feitoria
MODERN PORTUGUESE €€€

11 Map p82, B4

João Rodrigues plays up Portuguese produce and oriental touches at this slick, contemporary Michelin-starred restaurant overlooking the riverfront. Rich textures and clean, bright flavours dominate. You might start, say, with sautéed Algarve scarlet shrimp with cucumber salad and tartar, followed by a main like meltingly tender suckling pig with blood orange, pumpkin and tiger prawns. Excellent wines. (☎210 400 200; www.restaurantefeitoria.com; Altis Belém Hotel, Doca do Bom Sucesso; mains €28-39, tasting menus €70-155; ⏱7.30-11pm Mon-Sat)

Drinking

Bar 38° 41'   BAR

12 🍷 Map p82, B4

Watch boats bob on the water over coffee or cocktails at this stylish dockside lounge bar. Guest DJs liven things up on Friday nights and the bar occasionally hosts live jazz. (Altis Belém Hotel, Doca do Bom Sucesso; ⏱11am-1am)

Bar Terraço   BAR, CAFE

13 🍷 Map p82, B3

Revive museum-weary eyes at Bar Terraço on the upper level of CCB. The river-facing terrace is an attractive spot for sipping a cold one. Snacks and light meals are also served. (www.ccb.pt; Praça do Império, CCB; ⏱12.30-8pm Mon-Fri, 10am-7pm Sat)

Entertainment

Centro Cultural de Belém   THEATRE

14 ⭐ Map p82, B3

CCB presents a diverse program spanning experimental jazz, contemporary ballet, boundary-crossing plays and performances by the Portuguese Chamber Orchestra. (CCB; ☎213 612 400; www.ccb.pt; Praça do Império)

Shopping

Original Lisboa   HANDICRAFTS

15 🔒 Map p82, D2

As its name suggests, this is the place to find original gifts by young Portuguese designers. Playful ceramic jewellery in candy-bright colours, bags emblazoned with Lisbon trams, cork creations, *azulejo* coasters, paintings and fashion – it's all at this one-stop shop. (Rua de Belém 80; ⏱11am-7.30pm Tue-Sun)

Arte Periférica   ARTS & CRAFTS

16 🔒 Map p82, B3

This gallery in CCB spotlights the work of young Portuguese artists, from abstract paintings to contemporary landscapes and portraits. Inspired? The store opposite stocks art supplies. (www.ccb.pt; CCB, Praça do Império; ⏱10am-8pm)

Margarida Pimentel   FASHION & ACCESSORIES

17 🔒 Map p82, C3

Margarida Pimentel's ultrafine, nature-inspired jewellery fuses silver and gold with semiprecious stones. The designer's squiggly necklaces and bangles make snazzy gifts. (CCB, Praça do Império; ⏱10am-9pm)

Explore

Parque das Nações

A shining model of urban regeneration, Parque das Nações has almost single-handedly propelled the city into the 21st century since Expo '98. Glittering high-rises, sci-fi concert halls and Europe's longest bridge and second-largest aquarium rise above a river so wide it could be the sea. This is the Lisbon of progressive architecture, public art, riverside gardens and cutting-edge ballet. This is the future.

The Sights in a Day

☀ Start at the Gare do Oriente (pictured left; p93). Brush away the cobwebs with a brisk morning walk along the riverfront promenade, studded with eye-catching **sculptures** (p94) by Antony Gormley, Jorge Vieira et al. The luxuriant botanical greenery of **Jardim Garcia de Orta** (p93) leads to the caravel-shaped **Torre Vasco da Gama** (p93). From here, the views of the seemingly infinite **Ponte Vasco da Gama** (p93) are breathtaking. Hitch a scenic ride back on the **Teleférico** (p95), before mooching across to **Bota Feijão** (p95) for a relaxed lunch.

☼ Cool off in the midday sun with water games in the **Jardins d'Água** (p95). Now you're ready for total immersion at the **Oceanário** (p90), Lisbon's monster-sized aquarium, where you'll come face-to-face with sea otters, sharks, penguins and more. Kids in tow? Squeeze in some science-focused fun at the **Pavilhão do Conhecimento** (p93).

☾ Wander down to the marina for an aperitif with a river view, before a sophisticated dinner and drinks at the slick, Tejo-facing **River Lounge** (p96). Round out the day with a ballet performance at **Teatro Camões** (p97), a concert at the UFO-shaped **Pavilhão Atlântico** (p96) or a flutter at **Casino Lisboa** (p97).

👁 Top Sights

Oceanário (p90)

🖤 Best of Lisbon

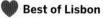

Azulejos

Gare do Oriente (p93)

Contemporary Art & Design

Street Art (p94)

For Kids

Oceanário (p90)

Pavilhão do Conhecimento (p93)

Jardins d'Água (p95)

Getting There

Ⓜ **Metro** The red line speeds you from central Lisbon to Gare do Oriente in around 20 minutes; services run frequently.

🚌 **Bus** Services connecting Parque das Nações to central Lisbon include the 708 to Martim Moniz (via the airport). Oriente is just three metro stops from the airport.

JOAO FIGUEIREDO/GETTY IMAGES ©

Top Sights
Oceanário

No amount of hype about Europe's second-largest aquarium – where 8000 species splash in 7 million litres of seawater – could ever convey the eye-popping scale of Lisbon's Oceanário. Sand tiger sharks, stingrays, pufferfish and sunfish can be spotted in the mammoth central tank, and puffins, penguins and sea otters in geographically focused exhibitions spotlighting the marine life of the North Atlantic, Antarctic, Pacific and tropical Indian Ocean. Conservation is the name of the game, with realistic habitats and no circus hoopla.

👁 Map p92, C4

www.oceanario.pt

Doca dos Olivais

adult/child €14/9

🕙10am-8pm

Don't Miss

Pacific Sea Otters

Make for the Pacific to coo over the Oceanário's superstar sea otters: Maré and Micas. The duo are ridiculously cute as they turn somersaults, swim placidly on their backs and groom their fur.

Central Tank

Standing in front of this whopper of a tank, or 'global ocean', is like scuba diving without getting wet. Speckled zebra sharks, globular sunfish, shoals of neon fish and manta rays – the flying carpets of the underwater world – hold audiences captive.

Sleeping with the Sharks

Who needs bedtime stories when you can scare your kids (and maybe yourself) silly by sleeping next to a shark tank? Costing €65 per person, these midnight Jaws encounters zoom in on conservation and give you the run of the almost-empty Oceanário the next morning.

Penguins on Ice

Watch Magellanic and crested rockhopper penguins waddle and slide across the ice in the Antarctic exhibition, then go down to the subaquatic level to glimpse them swimming gracefully underwater.

Underwater Close-Ups

Ghostlike moon jellyfish, giant octopuses, lacy sea dragons and big-belly sea horses are among the more unusual species splashing around in the tanks on the subaquatic level. Geeky fact for Nemo fans: clownfish are transsexual, with the dominant male eventually morphing into a female.

WESTEND61/GETTY IMAGES ©

☑ Top Tips

▶ Buy tickets online to jump the queue.

▶ Join a backstage tour for insight into what goes on behind the scenes.

▶ Don't use the flash on your camera – it frightens the fish.

▶ Pick up an audio guide for a running commentary of the exhibition.

▶ Plan your visit around feeding times: sea otters 10am, 12.45pm and 3.15pm; penguins 10am and 3pm; manta rays and sunfish 1pm; sharks 10.30am Monday and Friday; stingrays 11.15am Monday, Wednesday and Friday.

✖ Take a Break

The Oceanário's dazzlingly white, light-filled **cafe** (snacks & mains €5–€10) does appetising sandwiches and pastries and a fixed lunch menu for €9.80.

Take your pick of the riverside seafood restaurants along Rua da Pimenta.

A B C D

R Comandante Cousteau
11
1 Ponte Vasco da Gama

Av de Boa Esperança

Torre Vasco da Gama
5 13

8 Teleférico

7
Feira Internacional de Lisboa

4 Jardim Garcia de Orta

Av Dom João II

Alameda dos Oceanos

R da Pimenta

R do Bojador

10

15

R Conselheiro Lopo Vaz

6 Caminho da Água

16

Via Recíproca

Gare do Oriente Train Station

Gare do Oriente 2
Oriente M

19 Rossio dos Olivais

Av Berlim

Passeio das Tágides

Rio Tejo

Doca dos Olivais

18 12

Av Dom João II

Oceanário

3 Pavilhão do Conhecimento

Jardins d'Água 9

17

Passeio de Neptuno

Cabo Ruivo M

For reviews see

Top Sights	p90
Sights	p93
Eating	p95
Drinking	p96
Entertainment	p96
Shopping	p97

0 ——— 200 m
0 ——— 0.1 miles

Alameda dos Oceanos

Passeio do Adamastor

14

Sights

Ponte Vasco da Gama
BRIDGE

1 ⊚ Map p92, D1

Vanishing into a watery distance, Ponte Vasco da Gama is Europe's longest bridge, stretching 17.2km across the Rio Tejo. (Vasco da Gama Bridge)

Gare do Oriente
NOTABLE BUILDING

2 ⊚ Map p92, B3

Designed by acclaimed Spanish architect Santiago Calatrava, the space-age Gare do Oriente is an extraordinary vaulted structure, with slender columns fanning out into a concertina roof to create a kind of geometric, crystalline forest. (Oriente Station)

Pavilhão do Conhecimento
MUSEUM

3 ⊚ Map p92, C4

Kids won't grumble about science at the interactive Pavilhão do Conhecimento, where they can launch hydrogen rockets, lie unhurt on a bed of nails, experience the gravity on the moon and get dizzy on a high-wire bicycle. Budding physicists have fun whipping up tornadoes and blowing massive soap bubbles, while tots run riot in the adult-free unfinished house. (www.pavconhecimento.pt; Living Science Centre; adult/child €8/5; ⏱10am-6pm Tue-Fri, 11am-7pm Sat & Sun)

Jardim Garcia de Orta
GARDENS

4 ⊚ Map p92, D2

Bristling with exotic foliage from Portugal's former colonies, the Jardim Garcia de Orta is named after a 16th-century Portuguese naturalist and pioneer in tropical medicine. Botanical rarities include Madeira's bird of paradise and serpentine dragon tree.

Stroll the Brazilian garden, shaded by bougainvillea, silk-cotton, frangipani and tabasco pepper trees. There's also a music garden where kids can bash out melodies on giant triangles and gongs. (Garcia de Orta Garden; Rossio dos Olivais; admission free)

Torre Vasco da Gama
LANDMARK

5 ⊚ Map p92, D1

Shaped like the sail of explorer Vasco da Gama's mighty caravel, this 145m-high, concrete-and-steel skyscraper was designed by architects Leonor Janeiro and Nick Jacobs. Sidling up to the tower is the slick five-star Myriad by Sana Hotels, which opened in 2013 and bears the hallmark of architect Nuno Leónidas.

Caminho da Água
GARDENS

6 ⊚ Map p92, C3

Portuguese muralist Rigo designed this splash-happy boardwalk. Watch blue mosaic volcanoes erupt spontaneously or relax on one of the wave-shaped benches. Forget taking a dip, though, as bathing is forbidden. Well,

Understand

Progressive Art & Architecture

Metro Marvels

Gare do Oriente (p93) metro station became a showcase for Lisbon's boldest underground art at Expo '98 when it unveiled ocean-inspired sculptures and ceramic murals by internationally acclaimed artists. Be sure to glimpse Icelandic pop artist Erro's mythology-infused work depicting buxom mermaids and writhing octopuses, Austrian wild child Friedensreich Hundertwasser's technicolour cityscape *Submersão Atlântida* (Submersion of Atlantis), and Argentine postmodernist Antonio Seguí's playful mural featuring butch-looking mermaids and a sinking *Titanic*.

Street Art

Wandering along the riverfront promenades and gardens today, you'll see plenty of street art, including standouts by the much-lauded Antony Gormley (of *Angel of the North* fame) and the late Jorge Vieira.

As you exit Gare do Oriente, you'll be immediately struck by the eye-catching numbers on Rossio dos Olivais. One of these is **Rhizome**, Antony Gormley's abstract iron sculpture representing nine human figures that harmoniously slot together. Looking down, your gaze is drawn to **Mar Largo** by Fernando Conduto, an ocean-inspired pathway that reflects the tides of the Rio Tejo. Just a few steps away on Alameda dos Oceanos is the angular bulk of **Homem-Sol** (Sun Man), Jorge Vieira's 20m anthropomorphic iron-oxide giant. Most humorous, however, is **Lago das Tágides**, by Portuguese sculptor João Cutileiro, on Passeio das Tágides. These partially submerged marble sculptures of voluptuous nude women evoke poet Luís de Camões' mythical Tágides (nymphs of the Tagus).

Futuristic Architecture

Some of the world's most forward-thinking architects were drafted in to change the face of Parque das Nações for Expo '98, and they have left their indelible mark on the district. The theme was 'The Oceans, a Heritage for the Future', and this is reflected in some of the cutting-edge glass-and-steel edifices punctuating the waterfront. Most striking of all is the crystalline Gare do Oriente (p93) by Spain's star architect Santiago Calatrava, the flying saucer-shaped Pavilhão Atlântico (p96) by Portuguese architect Regino Cruz and the 145m-high Torre Vasco da Gama (p93), shaped like a caravel about to set sail, bearing the imprint of architects Leonor Janeiro, Nick Jacobs and SOM.

there's always the Tejo... (Water Path; Alameda dos Oceanos; admission free)

Feira Internacional de Lisboa
EXHIBITION CENTRE

7 ⊙ Map p92, C1

Designed by Portuguese architects Barreiros Ferreira and França Dória, the striking, crystalline FIL is Lisbon's premier venue for exhibitions and trade fairs. Check the website for details of upcoming events. (FIL; Lisbon International Fair; ☏218 921 500; www.fil.pt; Rua do Bojador; tickets free-€8)

Teleférico
CABLE CAR

8 ⊙ Map p92, D1

Hitch a ride on this 20m-high cable car linking Torre Vasco da Gama to the Oceanário. The ride affords bird's-eye views across Parque das Nações' skyline and the glittering Tejo that will have you burning up the pixels on your camera. (www.telecabinelisboa.pt; Passeio do Tejo; one-way adult/child €4/2; ⊗10.30am-8pm)

Jardins d'Água
WATER PARK

9 ⊙ Map p92, C4

These themed water gardens are a great spot to cool off in summer. When the sun shines, parents and their overexcited kids get soaked ducking behind the raging waterfalls and misty geysers, and testing out the hands-on water activities. (Water Gardens; Passeio de Neptuno; admission free; ⊗24hr)

Eating

Bota Feijão
PORTUGUESE €

10 ✕ Map p92, B2

Don't be fooled by the non-descript location and decor – when a tucked-away place is this crowded with locals at lunchtime midweek, it must be doing something right. They're all here for one thing and one thing only: *leitão*, suckling pig spit-roasted on an open fire until juicy and meltingly tender. (☏218 532 489; Rua Conselheiro Lopo Vaz 5; mains €7-15; ⊗8am-8pm Mon-Fri)

Il Pizzarium
PIZZERIA €

11 ✕ Map p92, C1

Facing the Torre Vasco da Gama, this neat little Italian job is a kid-friendly pit stop for pizza, pasta and gelato. There's a terrace for warm-day dining. (☏216 070 179; www.il-pizzarium.pt; Rua Comandante Cousteau Lote 4; pizza €6-15; ⊗11.30am-11pm; ▣)

☑ Top Tip

Free-Wheeling

With its expansive river views, parks and car-free promenades, Parque das Nações is a great place to get on your bike. You can rent reliable wheels at Bike Iberia (p30) in central Lisbon, a short stroll from Cais do Sodré. Besides standard bikes, it also has children's bikes, tandems and electric bikes.

Arrigato
JAPANESE €€€

12 Map p92, C4

Blonde wood and clean lines define this gallery-style restaurant. The buffet has an excellent variety of flavourful sushi and sashimi, and there's outdoor dining when the weather is nice. (☏ 218 967 132; Alameda dos Oceanos; lunch/dinner buffet €16/23; ⊗12.30-3pm & 7.30-11pm)

River Lounge
LOUNGE €€€

13 Map p92, D1

This slinky, monochrome, glass-walled restaurant-lounge has upped the style ante in Parque das Nações. Seasonal, Med-inspired cuisine is given a light touch of sophistication in dishes like sea bream with seaweed mash, oyster tartar and wild mushrooms in white-wine sauce. Perfect for pre- or after-dinner drinks, the terrace has stunning views of the Tejo and Ponte Vasco da Gama. (☏ 211 107 600; www.myriad.pt; Myriad by Sana Hotel, Cais das Naus; mains €18-30; ⊗7am-2am)

Drinking

Copo 5
WINE BAR

14 Map p92, D5

It's all about the view at this riverfront wine bar, where you can toast a fine sunset with a glass of Portuguese white or red and appetising *petiscos* (tapas). (Passeio dos Navegadores 6, Edifício Nau; ⊗noon-2am)

República da Cerveja
BAR

15 Map p92, D2

The service and food can be hit or miss at this bar, but it remains one of the liveliest spots for a pint of Guinness along the waterfront. Come for the river views, good beer selection and occasional gig. (Passeio das Tágides; ⊗12.30pm-1am)

Entertainment

Pavilhão Atlântico
CONCERT VENUE

16 Map p92, C3

Sporting an energy-efficient zinc roof, this UFO-shaped arena is Portugal's largest, hosting big international acts from Moby to Madonna. (☏ 218 918 409; www.pavilhaoatlantico.pt; Parque das Nações)

> ### ☑ Top Tip
>
> **Eat Streets**
>
> Brazilian, Italian, Indian, Thai, Portuguese – Parque das Nações serves up the world on a plate. Rather than book ahead, you can simply take a stroll along the riverfront and see what grabs you. Restaurants with alfresco seating abound on Passeio das Tágides and Alameda dos Oceanos, many of them offering good-value fixed lunch menus for less than €10. If you're eating on the hoof, try the Centro Vasco da Gama shopping mall (p97), with its snack bars, sushi outlets and cafes.

ROLHAS – PEDRO DAMÁSIO/GETTY IMAGES ©

Ponte Vasco da Gama (p93)

Teatro Camões
BALLET

17 ⭐ Map p92, C5

Teatro Camões is home to the Portuguese National Ballet Company under the artistic direction of Luísa Taveira. (☎218 923 477; www.cnb.pt; Parque das Nações)

Casino Lisboa
CASINO

18 ⭐ Map p92, C4

The sibling rival of Estoril, Lisbon's slick casino aims its chips at a younger crowd. Forget the James Bond–style tux, the dress code here is smart casual. Aside from 1000 slot machines, 22 gaming tables and three restaurants, the casino hosts concerts and circus acts in the revolving Arena Lounge.

Branded a white elephant when it opened in 2006, the casino has played its cards right recently to boost its popularity. (☎218 929 000; www.casino-lisboa.pt; Alameda dos Oceanos; ☺3pm-3am Sun-Thu, 4pm-4am Fri & Sat)

Shopping

Centro Vasco da Gama
MALL

19 🅿 Map p92, C3

Glass-roofed mall sheltering high-street stores, cinema and a food court – upper-level restaurants have outdoor seating with a view. (www.centrovascodagama.pt; Parque das Nações; ☺9am-midnight)

Explore

Marquês de Pombal, Rato & Saldanha

Some of Lisbon's finest restaurants, designer boutiques and concert halls make it easy to fill an entire day in this northern swathe of the city. Beyond the tree-fringed Avenida da Liberdade lie graceful art-nouveau houses, manicured gardens and galleries showcasing artists from Paula Rego to Rembrandt. High culture and good living are what these modern neighbourhoods are all about.

The Sights in a Day

☀ Begin your day with a classic saunter along Avenida da Liberdade, hanging out with style-conscious Lisboetas in boutiques like the **Fashion Clinic** (p109) and stopping at one of the kiosks for a people-watching cuppa. Get cityscape views from the heights of **Parque Eduardo VII** (pictured left: p104), before continuing to the **Estufas** (p104) greenhouses, bristling with tree ferns, mango trees and cacti.

☀ Hop on the metro to Saldanha, a short amble from **Versailles** (p105), where cream cakes and pastries are served in gilt and stucco surrounds. Your afternoon is going to be an arty one. Set aside a couple of hours to do justice to the Old Master paintings and Egyptian treasures in the **Museu Calouste Gulbenkian** (p100), then wander through the gardens to its contemporary neighbour – the **Centro de Arte Moderna** (p104).

☾ Toast the start of your evening with cocktails and stunning Lisbon views at the rooftop **Sky Bar** (p108), before dinner in the romantic courtyard at the **Casa da Comida** (p106) or at playfully modern **Assinatura** (p106). A concert at the **Fundação Calouste Gulbenkian** (p108) or an evening sipping wine in the vaults of Lisbon's aqueduct at **Chafariz do Vinho** (p108) rounds out the day nicely.

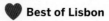

👁 Top Sights

Museu Calouste Gulbenkian (p100)

💜 Best of Lisbon

Food

Avenue (p107)

Assinatura (p106)

Casa da Comida (p106)

Os Tibetanos (p105)

Viewpoints

Sky Bar (p108)

Museums

Museu Calouste Gulbenkian (p100)

Casa-Museu Medeiros e Almeida (p104)

Getting There

Ⓜ **Metro** Though attractions are spread out, the metro makes getting around a breeze. Handy stops include Avenida, Marquês de Pombal, Rato, São Sebastião and Parque on the yellow and blue lines. If you're visiting more than one place, invest in a 24-hour Carris/metro pass.

🚍 **Bus** The AeroBus stops at Marquês de Pombal and Avenida da Liberdade en route to/from the airport.

Top Sights
Museu Calouste Gulbenkian

The Museu Calouste Gulbenkian showcases an epic collection of Western and Eastern art famous for its outstanding quality and breadth. You can easily spend half a day taking a chronological tour of the treasures that wealthy Armenian art collector Calouste Sarkis Gulbenkian (1869–1955) picked up on his world travels. Egyptian pharaoh reliefs, Persian carpets, Qing porcelain, 18th-century French silver, Dutch Master paintings, impressionist art and exquisite René Lalique jewellery – this is an exuberant feast of fine and decorative arts.

◉ Map p102, B2

www.museu.gulbenkian.pt

Avenida de Berna 45

adult/child €5/free

🕙10am-6pm Tue-Sun

Don't Miss

Dutch & Flemish Masters

Old Master enthusiasts are in their element contemplating 17th-century masterpieces such as Rembrandt's chiaroscuro *Portrait of an Old Man* and Rubens' frantic *Loves of the Centaurs* and biblical *Flight into Egypt.* Ruisdael's stormy Norwegian scenes and van Dyck portraits star among other highlights.

René Lalique

An entire room spotlights the impossibly intricate glassware and jewellery of French art-nouveau designer René Lalique. Marvel at his naturalistic diadems, hair combs, chalices and bracelets, bejewelled with baroque pearls and opals.

19th-Century Fine Art

This collection zooms in on French and English masterpieces like Manet's *Boy Blowing Bubbles,* Monet's *Break-Up of the Ice* and Turner's *Wreck of a Transport Ship.* Look, too, for impressionistic Degas portraits, Theodore Rousseau landscapes and Rodin's *Eternal Spring* sculpture.

Egyptian & Greco-Roman Art

With its gilded mummy mask, bronze cats and bas-relief pharaohs, the Egyptian collection provides a fascinating insight into this chapter of history. Next is the Greco-Roman room, displaying Greek coins and medallions, Roman glass and ceramics.

Islamic Art

Be captivated by the rich hues and geometric patterns of the museum's Persian carpets, kilims and brocaded silk – many dating to the 15th and 16th centuries. These feature alongside Ottoman faience, ornate tiles and Egyptian mosque lamps.

☑ Top Tips

▶ Visit on Sunday when entry to the permanent collection is free.

▶ Once a month at noon on Sunday, the gallery hosts a free recital in the foyer.

▶ See the website for special events aimed at kids and families.

▶ Learn more about the works on display with an audio guide.

✗ Take a Break

Grab a bite to eat in the museum **cafe** (snacks & mains €3–10), which has a pleasant patio for sunny days and a decent menu of soups, sandwiches and daily specials.

For something sweet, take a stroll to the gloriously old-world Versailles (p105) patisserie nearby.

400 m
0.25 miles

R Alves Redol

Pç da Ilha
do Faial

ESTEFÂNIA

R Dona

R da Escola
de Medicina
Veterinária

R do Arco do Cego

R Dona Filipa de Vilhena

R Dona Estefânia

22

R Dona Almeida

Av Praia
da Vitória

R Fernão
Lopes

R Casal Ribeiro

R Actor
Taborda

R Almirante
Barroso

Av dos Defensores

R António José de Chaves

SALDANHA

Saldanha

Pç do Duque
de Saldanha

R Engenheiro

Campo
Pequeno

Av da República

Av da Barbosa du Bocage

Av Duque d'Ávila

8

Picoas

Av Elias Garcia

Av da Barbosa du Bocage

Av 5 de Outubro

Melo

Av 5 de Outubro

Av Marquês de Tomar

Av Visconde Valmour

Av Miguel Bombarda

R António Enes

R Filipe Folque

R Latino Coelho

R Pedro Nunes

R Tomás Ribeiro

R Virato

Av de Berna

Av Conde de Valbom

R João Crisóstomo

R Pinheiro Chagas

R São Sebastião de Pedreira

Parque

Av Sidónio Pais

R Marquês de Sa Bandeira

R D António Cândido

Av Luís Bivar

R Luís Bivar

Museu Calouste
Gulbenkian

Centro de
Arte Moderna

19

1

R Dr. Nicolau de Bettencourt

Av António Augusto de Aguiar

25

Jardim
Amália
Rodrigues

Av Santos Dumont

São Sebastião

R Ramalho Ortigão

Alameda Cardeal Cerejeira

R Marquês da Fronteira

Pç de
Espanha

SETE
RIOS

Av Columbano
Bordalo

Praça
Espanha

Av Calouste Gulbenkian

CAMPOLIDE

Estefânia

R Gomes Freire

R Gonçalves Crespo

R Luciano Cordeiro

R de Santo António

Campo dos
Mártires
da Pátria

R das
Portas de
Santo Antão

18

15

Restauradores

R Bernardim Ribeiro

R do Pasadiço

R dos
Condes

28

R do Telhal

R Andrade
Corvo

R do Conde de Redondo

R de Santa Marta

R de São José

24

R da
Conceição

10

R da Glória

Av Duque de Loulé

R Rodrigues Sampaio

Avenida

14

Pç da
Alegria

21

R da Glória

17

Av Fontes Pereira de

R Camilo Castelo Branco

Marquês de
Pombal

Casa-Museu
Medeiros e
Almeida

11

9

2

R da
Alegria

R Mãe
d'Água

Av da Liberdade

16

7

Salitre

R da Salitre

20

27

R Duque
de Palmela

R Rosa Araújo

R Barata

Jardim
Botânico

5

Parque
Eduardo VII

3

R Mouzinho
da Silveira

R Alexandre Herculano

R do Vale
Pereiro

13

R da Escola Politécnica

R Gustavo de
Matos Sequeira

4

Estufas

R de Joaquim António Aguiar

R Castilho

RATO

R S Felipe Nery

23

R da São
Mamede

Alameda Edgar Cardoso

R Castilho

R Artilharia 1

Tv das
Amoreiras

Rato

R do Arco à
São Mamede

R de São Bento

R Rodrigo da Fonseca

R Artilharia 1

Pç das
Amoreiras

6

12

R Mãe
d'Água

Lg do Rato

Av Duarte
Pacheco

R das Amoreiras

R Dom João V

R do Sol ao Rato

26

R Artilharia 1

Sights

Centro de Arte Moderna
MUSEUM

1 ⊙ Map p102, B3

Situated in a sculpture-dotted garden alongside Museu Calouste Gulbenkian, the Centro de Arte Moderna reveals a stellar collection of 20th-century Portuguese and international art.

The collection stars works by David Hockney, Antony Gormley and José de Almada Negreiros. Feast your eyes on gems like Paula Rego's warped fairy-tale series *Contos Populares* and Sonia Delaunay's geometrically bold *Chanteur Flamenco*. There's also a well-stocked bookshop and garden cafe. (Modern Art Centre; www.cam.gulbenkian.pt; Rua Dr Nicaulau de Bettencourt; adult/chilld €5/free; ⊙10am-6pm Tue-Sun)

Casa-Museu Medeiros e Almeida
MUSEUM

2 ⊙ Map p102, C7

Housed in a stunning art-nouveau mansion, this little-known museum presents António Medeiros e Almeida's exquisite fine- and decorative-arts collection. Highlights include 18th-century Flemish tapestries, Qing porcelain, Thomas Gainsborough paintings, wondrous mechanised clocks and pendulums, and a dinner service that once belonged to Napoleon Bonaparte. (www.casa-museumedeirosealmeida.pt; Rua Rosa Araújo 41; adult/child €5/free; ⊙1-5.30pm Mon-Sat)

☑️ Top Tip

Free Museum & Gallery Entry

Save museum and gallery visits for the weekend. Museu Calouste Gulbenkian and Centro de Arte Moderna both offer free entry on Sundays, while the Casa-Museu Medeiros e Almeida is gratis from 10am to 1pm on Saturdays.

Parque Eduardo VII
PARK

3 ⊙ Map p102, C5

An urban oasis with British roots, Parque Eduardo VII is named after his highness Edward VII, who visited Lisbon in 1903. The sloping parterre affords sweeping views over the whizzing traffic of Praça Marquês de Pombal to the river. (Alameda Edgar Cardoso; admission free; ⊙daylight hours)

Estufas
GARDENS

4 ⊙ Map p102, B5

Tucked away in a pocket of Parque Eduardo VII, this trio of glasshouses nurtures tree ferns and camellias in the *estufa fría* (cool greenhouse), coffee and mango trees in the *estufa quente* (hot greenhouse) and cacti in the *estufa doce* (sweet greenhouse). (Greenhouses; http://estufafria.cm-lisboa.pt; adult/child €3.10/2.30, Sun 9am-2pm free; ⊙10am-7pm Apr-Oct, 9am-5pm Nov-Mar)

Jardim Botânico GARDENS

5 ⊙ Map p102, C8

Nurtured by green-fingered students, the Jardim Botânico is a quiet pocket of lushness just north of Bairro Alto. Look out for Madeiran geraniums, sequoias, purple jacarandas and, by the entrance (upper level gardens), a gigantic Moreton Bay fig tree. It's also worth a peek inside the butterfly house. (Botanical Garden; www.mnhnc.ulisboa.pt; Rua da Escola Politécnica 58; adult/child €2/1; ⊙gardens 9am-8pm, butterfly house 11am-5pm Tue-Fri, 11am-6pm Sat & Sun)

Mãe d'Água HISTORIC BUILDING

6 ⊙ Map p102, B7

The king laid the aqueduct's final stone at Mãe d'Água, the city's massive 5500-cu-metre main reservoir. Completed in 1834, the reservoir's cool, echoing chamber is a fine place to admire 19th-century technology. Climb the stairs for a fine view of the aqueduct and the surrounding neighbourhood. (Mother of Water; Praça das Amoreiras 10; adult/child €3/1.50; ⊙10am-5.30pm Tue-Sat)

Eating

Os Tibetanos VEGETARIAN €

7 ✕ Map p102, D7

Part of a Tibetan Buddhism school the mantra here is fresh vegetarian food, with daily specials such as quiche and curry. Sit in the serene courtyard if the sun's out and save room for rosepetal ice cream. (⊡213 142 038; Rua do Salitre 117; mains €7-10; ⊙12.45-2.45pm & 7.30-10.30pm Mon-Sat; ✐)

Versailles PATISSERIE €

8 ✕ Map p102, D3

With a marble chandelier and icing-sugar stucco confection, this sublime patisserie is where well-coiffed ladies come to devour cream cakes (or scones with jam) and gossip. (⊡213 546 340; Avenida da República 15A; pastries €2-4; ⊙7.30am-10pm)

Understand
Aqueduct of the Free Waters

The 109 arches of the Aqueduto das Águas Livres lope across the hills into Lisbon from Caneças, more than 18km away; they are most spectacular at Campolide, where the tallest arch is an incredible 65m high. Built between 1728 and 1835, by order of Dom João V, the aqueduct is a spectacular feat of engineering and brought Lisbon its first clean drinking water. Its more sinister claim to fame is as the site where 19th-century mass murderer Diogo Alves pushed his victims over the edge. No prizes for guessing why it was closed to the public soon after.

Cinemateca Portuguesa

CAFE €

Hidden on the 2nd floor of the indie-loving cinema (see 20 ⭐ Map p102, C7), this bright, wood-filled cafe with its sunny terrace makes a fine retreat for an afternoon or evening pick-me-up. Menu features light snacks, drinks and daily specials. (Rua Barata Salgueiro 39; mains €6-8; ⏱12.30pm-1am Mon-Sat)

Cervejaria Ribadouro

SEAFOOD €€

9 🍴 Map p102, D7

Bright, noisy and full to the gills, this bustling beer hall is popular with the local seafood fans. The shellfish are plucked fresh from the tank, weighed and cooked to lip-smacking perfection. (☎213 549 411; Rua do Salitre 2; mains €10-28, prawns/lobster per kg from €41/76; ⏱noon-1.30am)

As Velhas

PORTUGUESE €€

10 🍴 Map p102, D8

No airs, no graces, just hearty help-ings of Portuguese soul food and smiles are what to expect at this beamed restaurant. The monkfish and clams in garlic and coriander sauce is superb. (☎213 422 490; Rua da Conceição da Glória 21; mains €12-28; ⏱noon-3pm & 7-10.30pm Mon-Fri, 7-10.30pm Sat)

Guilty

INTERNATIONAL €€

11 🍴 Map p102, C7

Midway between restaurant and club-by lounge bar, Guilty is the latest of Lisbon master chef Olivier's ventures.

With its bare brick walls, leather sofas, cowhides and young, good-looking crowd, it's sexy and it knows it, but this is the place to come for Wagyu burgers, pasta, speciality piz-zas and DJ beats. Service can be hit or miss. (☎211 913 590; www.restaurante-olivier.com; Rua Barata Salgueiro 28A; mains €12-38; ⏱noon-3.30pm & 7.30pm-1am)

Casa da Comida

PORTUGUESE €€€

12 🍴 Map p102, B7

A gorgeous blend of the historic and the contemporary, Casa da Comida has a dash of design and a generous pinch of Portuguese soul. *Azulejo* panels, revamped antique chairs and clever backlighting set the scene for chef Miguel Carvalho's season-inflected taste sensations, along the lines of roasted turbot with raspberry, celery purée and passion-fruit sauce. (☎213 885 376, 213 860 889; www.casadacomida.pt; Travessa das Amoreiras 1; mains €17-26; ⏱1-3pm & 8pm-midnight Tue-Sat, 8pm-midnight Mon)

Assinatura

MODERN PORTUGUESE €€€

13 🍴 Map p102, C7

Assinatura serves modern Portuguese food against a playful backdrop of backlit chandeliers and blown-up photos of Lisbon. The chef keeps it delightfully simple in mains such as monkfish wrapped in bacon and shell-fish *caldeirada* (stew). (☎213 867 696; www.assinatura.com.pt; Rua do Vale Pereiro 19; mains €26-35; ⏱12.30-3pm & 7.30-11pm Tue-Fri, 7.30-11pm Mon & Sat)

Centro de Arte Moderna (p104)

Avenue
INTERNATIONAL €€€

14 ✖ Map p102, D8

This glass-walled restaurant goes for the pared-down chic look. Service is as polished as the decor and the food emphasises Portuguese ingredients like *bacalhau* (dried salt-cod) and suckling pig, which are creatively prepared and served with an artistic flourish. The three-course lunch is great value at €20. (☎216 017 127; www.avenue.pt; Avenida da Liberdade 129B; mains €27-29, tasting menus €45-75; ⏱12.30-3pm & 7.30-11pm Mon-Fri, 7.30-11.30pm Sat)

Solar dos Presuntos
PORTUGUESE €€€

15 ✖ Map p102, E8

Don't be fooled by the smoked *presunto* (ham) hanging in the window, this iconic restaurant is renowned for its excellent seafood – as well as its smoked and grilled meats. There's a pleasant buzz to the folksy and welcoming space, with photos of admirers lining the restaurant's walls. Prawn and lobster curry, salt-baked sea bass and delectable seafood paella are among the top choices. (☎213 424 253; Rua das Portas de Santo Antão 150; mains €15-28; ⏱12.30-3.30pm & 7-11pm Mon-Sat)

Drinking

Sky Bar
BAR

16 🚇 Map p102, D7

Wow, what a view! This high-rise bar at the Tivoli has a gorgeous terrace, full of cushioned nooks for cocktail sipping, conversing and drinking in the panorama of Lisbon. (Tivoli Lisboa, Avenida da Liberdade 185; ⏰5pm-1am May-Sep)

Chafariz do Vinho
WINE BAR

17 🚇 Map p102, D8

In the centuries-old vaults of Lisbon's aqueduct, this beautiful *enoteca* (wine bar) pops the cork on wines hand-picked by writer João Paulo Martins. Taste Portugal's finest, from Alentejo whites to Douro reds. Depending on the wines, a four-glass tasting costs between €10 and €15. (www.chafarizdovinho. com; Rua Mãe d'Água; ⏰6pm-2am Tue-Sun)

Primeiro Andar
BAR

18 🚇 Map p102, E8

Although it's right above a touristy pedestrian street, this delightful cafe and bar remains well-concealed from the masses. Don't be shy, it's a welcoming, laid-back place, good for a pick-me-up in the afternoon (or an inexpensive meal) and drinks with friends by night.

To get there, take the small alley about 30m south of the Ateneu Comerical de Lisboa building, go to the end and head inside the dark entrance. (Ateneu Comerical de Lisboa, Rua das Portas de Santo Antão 110; ⏰7pm-2am)

Entertainment

Fundação Calouste Gulbenkian
MUSIC

19 ⭐ Map p102, B2

Home to the Gulbenkian Orchestra, this classical-music heavyweight stages first-rate concerts and ballets. (📞217 823 000; www.musica.gulbenkian.pt; Avenida de Berna 45A)

Cinemateca Portuguesa
CINEMA

20 ⭐ Map p102, C7

Screens offbeat, art-house, world and old films. (www.cinemateca.pt; Rua Barata Salgueiro 39)

Hot Clube de Portugal
JAZZ

21 ⭐ Map p102, D8

As hot as its name suggests, this small, poster-plastered cellar has staged top-drawer jazz acts since the 1940s. (📞213 619 740; www.hcp.pt; Praça da Alegria 48; ⏰10pm-2am Tue-Sat)

Culturgest
PERFORMING ARTS

22 ⭐ Map p102, E1

Culturgest's experimental and occasionally provocative line-up encompasses exhibitions, dance, poetry, music and theatre. (📞217 905 155; www.culturgest.pt; Rua do Arco do Cego; admission €5-14)

Shopping

Galeria de Arte São Mamede
ARTS & CRAFTS

23 🔒 Map p102, C8

Interesting to browse even if you have no intention of buying, this vaulted gallery displays the contemporary work of Portuguese artists. (www.saomamede.com; Rua da Escola Politécnica 167; ⏱10am-8pm Mon-Fri, 11am-7pm Sat)

Fashion Clinic
FASHION

24 🔒 Map p102, D7

Everything designer divas crave: ready-to-wear DKNY, Gucci and Prada, Jimmy Choo shoes, perfumes, accessories, fashion books and more. (www.fashionclinic.pt; Avenida da Liberdade 192; ⏱10am-7.30pm Mon-Sat)

El Corte Inglês
MALL

25 🔒 Map p102, B3

Spanish giant with nine floors of fashion, design and food. (www.elcorteingles.pt; Avenida António Augusto de Aguiar 31; ⏱10am-10pm Mon-Thu, 10am-11.30pm Fri & Sat, 10am-8pm Sun)

Complexo das Amoreiras
MALL

26 🔒 Map p102, A6

Modernist mall with 238 stores. (www.amoreiras.com; Avenida Duarte Pacheco; ⏱10am-11pm)

Local Life

Exploring the Avenida

Paris has the Champs-Élysées, London Regent St and Lisbon the tree-fringed **Avenida da Liberdade**. The 19th-century avenue is a mile-long ribbon of style, linking Praça dos Restauradores in the south to the busy Marquês de Pombal roundabout in the north. This is Lisbon's classic strolling boulevard, flanked by some of the city's chicest hotels and cafes and designer boutiques like Prada, Louis Vuitton, Fly London and Hugo Boss.

Break up your shopping with a stop at one of six kiosks, with tables set up under the trees, which do smoothies, wraps, hot dogs, chocolate cake and drinks. All are open from 10am to 2am.

Livraria Buchholz
BOOKS

27 🔒 Map p102, C6

Livraria Buchholz stocks one of Lisbon's meatiest collections of art books and English, French and German fiction. (Rua Duque de Palmela 4; ⏱9.30am-7.30pm Mon-Fri, 10am-2pm Sat)

Carbono
MUSIC

28 🔒 Map p102, E8

The staff may be grumpy, but it's hard not to like Carbono, with its impressive selection of new and secondhand vinyl and CDs. World music – West African boogaloo, Brazilian tropicalia – is especially well represented. (Rua do Telhal 6B; ⏱11am-7pm Mon-Sat)

Explore

Estrela, Lapa & Alcântara

In quiet, tree-lined Estrela and Lapa you can easily tiptoe off the well-trodden trail along cafe-rimmed squares, lanes with breezy river views and gentrified streets where 18th-century mansions harbour antique stores, boutiques and galleries. Down by the river, the Doca de Santo Amaro signals a new age for Lisbon: its once-industrial warehouses have been reborn as en-vogue bars, clubs and restaurants.

The Sights in a Day

☼ Launch your day with a nostalgic rumble through Lisbon on **tram 28** (p56), hopping off at the neoclassical **Basílica da Estrela** (pictured left; p116). Admire the basilica's ornate marble interior and scale the dome for broad city views. Then go for a botanical wander in the **Jardim da Estrela** (p116) opposite. Mooch around the antique shops and galleries on Rua de São Bento, before a deli-style lunch with a dash of the Alentejo at **O Cocho** (p118).

☼ Walk or take a quick tram ride to Lapa, lingering to soak up the neighbourly vibe in its steep, leafy backstreets. Contemplate art treasures in the palatial **Museu Nacional de Arte Antiga** (p112), then revive museum-weary eyes over a coffee and dazzling river views at **Le Chat** (p119). Tap into Lisbon's cutting-edge design scene at the **LX Factory** (p117), occupying a former textile factory. On Sunday you can bag vintage, craft and food finds at its market.

☽ Arrive at the Doca de Santo Amaro in time to see the **Ponte 25 de Abril** (p116) light up and the riverfront cafe and restaurant terraces hum with life. Head to **Cantinho Lusitano** (p118) for tapas expertly paired with Portuguese wines, or book a table at buzzy bistro **Frade dos Mares** (p118).

👁 Top Sights

Museu Nacional de Arte Antiga (p112)

🖤 Best of Lisbon

Churches, Castles & Palaces
Basílica da Estrela (p116)

Contemporary Art & Design
LX Factory (p117)

Food
Frade dos Mares (p118)

Clube das Jornalistas (p118)

Cafe de São Bento (p118)

Museums
Museu Nacional de Arte Antiga (p112)

Museu do Oriente (p116)

Getting There

🚋 **Tram** Tram 15 from Praça da Figueira and tram 18 from Cais do Sodré reach Santos and Alcântara. Tram 25 trundles to Santos, Lapa and Estrela. Tram 28 is also convenient for Estrela.

🚌 **Bus** Buses 713 (Arco do Cego–Estação Campolide) and 727 (Estação Roma–Areeiro–Restelo) stop in Estrela, Lapa and Alcântara. Bus 712 is useful for Alcântara.

Top Sights
Museu Nacional de Arte Antiga

On its scenic perch above the river, this 17th-century palace, once home to the Counts of Alvor, is a fittingly grand backdrop for Lisbon's foremost collection of ancient art. And what a collection it is! Meissen porcelain, Portuguese sculpture, Beauvais tapestry, Ming porcelain, baroque silverware and Japanese screens do a stellar job of whisking you through the world of fine and decorative arts from the Middle Ages to the 19th century. Keep an eye out for star pieces by Albrecht Dürer, Nuno Gonçalves and Gil Vicente.

Ancient Art Museum

◉ Map p114, F4

www.museudearte-antiga.pt

Rua das Janelas Verdes

adult/child €6/3, 1st Sun of the month free

🕑 2-6pm Tue, 10am-6pm Wed-Sun

Don't Miss

Panels of St Vincent

Covering an entire wall (room 12; 3rd floor), the *Panels of St Vincent* are the museum's pride and joy. Attributed to Nuno Gonçalves, the painter of King Afonso V, and dating to 1470, the expressive polyptych depicts the veneration of St Vincent.

Monstrance & Cross

The gold and silverware collection's two stand-outs hide in room 29. First up is Gil Vicente's golden wonder, the monstrance of Belém (1506), made from the gold brought back from Vasco da Gama's second voyage to India, and embellished with armillary spheres and the 12 apostles. Just as dazzling is the 1214 processional cross of King Sancho I, delicately engraved and bejewelled with pearls and sapphires.

European Painting

Strong on ecclesiastical painting, this collection takes a blockbuster tour of 14th- to 19th-century European art. Two pieces in particular stand out. The first is a Renaissance masterpiece, Albrecht Dürer's chiaroscuro *St Jerome* (1521). The second is Jheronimus Bosch's devotional triptych, *St Anthony* (1500), an evocative depiction of the hermit being attacked by demons and faced with sins like gluttony and abandonment of the faith.

Oriental Art & Ceramics

Exquisite 16th-century Indian caskets inlaid with mother of pearl, Ming porcelain and geometric tiles from Syria and Turkey all beg exploration on the 2nd floor. Be sure to see the beautifully gilded Namban screens, depicting the arrival of the Namban (southern barbarians), the Portuguese explorers who arrived in Japan in 1543 and shocked locals with their uncouth behaviour.

☑ **Top Tips**

▶ On a budget? Visit on a Sunday when entry is free from 10am to 2pm.

▶ This museum is simply huge, so pick up a map at the entrance to pinpoint what you really want to see. Allow a minimum of two hours.

▶ Arrive early or late to dodge the crowds.

✖ **Take a Break**

Step next door to Le Chat (p119) for drinks and snacks on a terrace with captivating river views.

For a more traditional Portuguese lunch, try nearby **O Caldo Verde** (Map p114, G3; ☑ 213 903 581; Rua da Esperança 89; mains €6-21; ⊙11.30am-3.30pm & 7.30pm-midnight). Despite the name alluding to cabbage soup, steak cooked to perfection is the big deal here.

A B C D

1

2

3

4

5

Parque Florestal
de Monsanto

Av da Ponte

Av de Ceuta

ALCÂNTARA

Acesso a Ponte

Tapada
da Ajuda

Tapada das
Necessidades

Cç das Necessidades

Pç Gen de
Domingos
Oliveira

Cç da Tapada

R dos Lusíadas

R de Alcântara

R João de
Oliveira
Miguens

R Prior do Crato

R do Arco

Av Infante Santo

Lg do
Calvario

R Primeiro de Maio

R Rodrigues
de Faria

R de Cascais

Av 24 de Julho

Av da Índia

25

Av da Índia

1 Museu do
Oriente

Alcântara-Mar
Train Station

Av da Ponte

Av de Brasília

Doca de
Santo Amaro

Av da Índia

3 Ponte 25
de Abril

E

7 British Cemetery
R de São Jorge

F

Jardim da Estrela
5

G

Casa Museu de Amália Rodrigues
9
R de Santo Amaro
8
R de São Bento
10
R dos Prazeres

H

20
Tv Santa Teresa

R do Patrocínio
18

R da Estrela

2 Basílica da Estrela

ESTRELA

Pç da Estrela

R de São Bento

R da Imprensa

Palácio da Assembleia da República
13
4

Cç da Estrela

R Academia Ciências

Lg de Jesus

Av Infante Santo

R de Sant'ana a Lapa

R de São Domingos

R de Buenos Aires

R dos Navegantes

R da Bela Vista a Lapa

R de Borges Caneiro

R dos Polais de São Bento

R do Poço dos Negros

Tv Alcaide

R da Lapa

R do Meio à Lapa

22

R do Quelhas

11

R dos Trinas

R dos Remedios

R dos Prazeres

MADRAGOA

Museu da Marioneta

14

24

R da Silva

Av Dom Carlos I

23

R da Boavista

Lg do Conde Barão

R Dom Luis I

LAPA

R Garcia da Horta

R do Conde

R de Santos-o-Velho

19

16

6

15

12

R da Esperança

Cç Marquês de Abrantes

Lg de Santos

R do Pau da Bandeira

R do Sacramento a Lapa

R Ribeiro Sanches

R das Janelas Verdes

Cç Ribeiro Santos

Av 24 de Julho

Santos Train Station

26

R do Olival

17

Museu Nacional de Arte Antiga

21

R Presidente Arriaga

Av 24 de Julho

Av de Brasília

Cais da Viscondessa

N
0   500 m
0   0.25 miles

Doca de Alcântara

Rio Tejo

Sights

Museu do Oriente
MUSEUM

1 ⊙ Map p114, C4

The beautifully designed Museu do Oriente highlights Portugal's ties with Asia, from colonial baby steps in Macau to ancestor worship. The cavernous museum occupies a revamped 1940s *bacalhau* (dried salt-cod) warehouse – a €30 million conversion. Strikingly displayed in pitch-black rooms, the permanent collection focuses on the Portuguese presence in Asia, and Asian gods.

Standouts on the 1st floor feature rare Chinese screens and Ming porcelain, plus East Timor curiosities such as the divining conch and delicately carved umbilical-cord knives. Upstairs, cult classics include peacock-feathered effigies of Yellamma (goddess of the fallen), Vietnamese medium costumes and an eerie, faceless Nepalese exorcism doll. (www.museudooriente.pt; Doca de Alcântara; adult/child €6/2, admission free 6-10pm Fri; ⊙10am-6pm Tue-Sun, to 10pm Fri)

Basílica da Estrela
CHURCH

2 ⊙ Map p114, F1

The curvaceous, sugar-white dome and twin belfries of Basílica da Estrela are visible from afar. The echoing interior is awash with pink-and-black marble, which creates a kaleidoscopic effect when you gaze up into the cupola. The neoclassical beauty was completed in 1790 by order of Dona Maria I (whose tomb is here) in gratitude for a male heir. (Praça da Estrela; basilica free, nativity scene €1.50, roof €4 ; ⊙7.30am-7.45pm)

Ponte 25 de Abril
BRIDGE

3 ⊙ Map p114, B5

Most people experience déjà vu the first time they clap eyes on bombastic suspension bridge Ponte 25 de Abril. It's hardly surprising given that it's the spitting image of San Francisco's Golden Gate Bridge – it was constructed by the same company in 1966, and, at 2.27km, is almost as long. (Doca de Santo Amaro)

Palácio da Assembleia da República
NOTABLE BUILDING

4 ⊙ Map p114, G2

The columned, temple-like Palácio da Assembleia da República (closed to the public) is where Portugal's parliament, the Assembleia da República, makes its home. It was once the enormous Benedictine Mosteiro de São Bento, and is decorated with lofty Doric columns and graceful statues of temperance, prudence, fortitude and justice. (Assembly of the Republic; Rua de São Bento)

Jardim da Estrela
GARDENS

5 ⊙ Map p114, F1

Seeking green respite? Opposite the Basílica da Estrela, this garden is perfect for a stroll, with paths weaving past pine, monkey puzzle and palm trees, rose and cacti beds and the centrepiece – a giant banyan tree. Kids love the duck ponds and animal-themed playground. There are several open-air cafes where you can recharge. (Largo da Estrela; admission free; ⊙gardens 7am-midnight, cafe 10am-11pm)

Museu da Marioneta MUSEUM

6 ◉ Map p114, G3

Discover your inner child at the enchanting Museu da Marioneta, a veritable Geppetto's workshop housed in the 17th-century Convento das Bernardas. Alongside superstars such as impish Punch and his Russian equivalent Petruschka are rarities: Vietnamese water puppets, Sicilian opera marionettes and intricate Burmese shadow puppets. (Puppet Museum; www.museudamarioneta.pt; Rua da Esperança 146; adult/child €5/3, free 10am-1pm Sun; ⊙10am-1pm & 2-6pm Tue-Sun)

British Cemetery CEMETERY

7 ◉ Map p114, F1

Overgrown with cypress trees, the Cemitério dos Ingleses was founded in 1717. Expats at rest here include Henry Fielding (author of *Tom Jones*), who died during a fruitless visit to Lisbon in 1754 to improve his health. At the far corner are the remains of Lisbon's old Jewish cemetery. (Rua de São Jorge; admission free; ⊙10.30am-1pm Mon-Fri)

Casa Museu de Amália Rodrigues MUSEUM

8 ◉ Map p114, G1

A pilgrimage site for fado fans, the Casa Museu de Amália Rodrigues is where the Rainha do Fado (Queen of Fado) Amália Rodrigues lived; note graffiti along the street announcing it as Rua Amália. Short tours take in portraits, glittering costumes and crackly recordings of her performances. (www.amaliarodrigues.pt; Rua de São Bento 193; adult/child €5/3.50; ⊙10am-1pm & 2-6pm Tue-Sun)

Local Life
LX Factory

Tune into Lisbon's creative pulse at the **LX Factory** (Map p114, B4; www.lxfactory.com; Rua Rodrigues de Faria 103, Alcântara), housed in a cavernous 19th-century textile factory. Some 23,000 sq metres of abandoned warehouses have been transformed into art studios, galleries, workshops and printing and design companies. Today LX Factory hosts a dynamic menu of events from live concerts and film screenings to fashion shows and art exhibitions. There's a rustically cool cafe as well as a restaurant, **Cantina** (mains €11-18.50; ⊙9am-3pm Mon, 9am-midnight Tue-Sat, 9am-4pm Sun), plus other design-minded shops. Weekend nights see parties with a dance-loving and art-loving crowd. Check website for events.

Eating

O Cocho – Mercearia Alentejana
DELI €

9   Map p114, G1

This sweet deli and grocery store plays up top-quality, sustainably sourced produce from the Alentejo. Wholesome soups, toasties, tapas and some of Lisbon's best *empadas* (pies) are on the menu. You can also pick up great edible gifts (wines, honeys, syrups and the like). (☎912 376 675; www.ococho.com; Rua de São Bento 239; snacks & light bites €2-10; ◷10am-8pm Mon-Sat)

Cantinho Lusitano
PORTUGUESE €

10   Map p114, H1

Sharing is what this unassuming little place is all about. Its appealing menu of *petiscos* (tapas), such as Azeitão cheese, chorizo, garlic shrimps, *pica-pau* beef and fava bean salad, pairs nicely with Portuguese wines. (☎218 065 185; www.cantinholusitano.com; Rua dos Prazeres 52; pestiscos €4-8.50; ◷7-11pm Tue-Sat)

Landeau
DESSERTS €

Landeau is quite simply about having your cake and eating it. The industro-cool cafe at the LX Factory (see 25 🔒 Map p114, B4) is famous for its dark, dense, deliciously moist chocolate cake. (www.landeau.pt; LX Factory, Rua Rodrigues de Faria 103; chocolate cake €3.50; ◷noon-7pm)

Clube das Jornalistas
MEDITERRANEAN €€

11   Map p114, F2

You have to be determined to find hilltop Clube das Jornalistas, but persevere. This 18th-century house, opening onto a tree-shaded courtyard, has oodles of charm and serves Med-style and Portuguese dishes like parrot fish with creamy lemon risotto and black pork with *feijoada* (bean stew). The service is faultless, the food superb. (☎213 977 138; Rua das Trinas 129; mains €13-22; ◷12.30-2.30pm & 7.30-10.30pm Mon-Sat)

Frade dos Mares
PORTUGUESE €€

12   Map p114, G3

This smart, contemporary bistro keeps the mood relaxed with soft lighting and unobtrusive service. The menu is simple – sirloin steak, grilled fish and the like – but everything is cooked to a T. Children and vegetarians are well catered for. (☎213 909 418; www.fradedosmares.com; Avenida Dom Carlos I 55; mains €13-19; ◷noon-3pm & 8-11.30pm Mon-Fri, 8-11.30pm Sat; 👶)

Cafe de São Bento
PORTUGUESE €€

13   Map p114, H1

This warm, convivial brasserie prides itself on just one dish: steak cooked to perfection, served with cream sauce, skinny fries and side orders like spinach and fried eggs. It hits the mark every time. (☎213 952 911; www.cafesaobento.com; Rua de São Bento 212; mains €17-23; ◷12.30-2.30pm & 7pm-2am Mon-Fri, 7pm-2am Sat & Sun)

Petiscaria Ideal

FUSION €€

14 🍴 Map p114, G3

This small buzzing spot serves up delicious *petiscos* – octopus with tomato sauce and sweet potatoes, black sausage with apple purée, and soft polenta with clams, followed by chocolate cake with fresh cream and wild berries. Walls are clad with mismatching *azulejos*, dining is at long communal tables, and there's a spirited rock-and-roll vibe to the place. (📞213 971 504; Rua da Esperança 100; small plates €9-11; ⏱7.30pm-midnight Tue-Sat)

Taberna Ideal

FUSION €€

15 🍴 Map p114, G3

In a cosy, atmospheric dining room, Taberna Ideal wows diners with flavourful dishes that blend Alentejan recipes with a modern edge. The inventive menu changes daily and features plates designed for sharing. Recent favourites include goat cheese, honey and rosemary bruschetta; braised pork; scrambled eggs with game sausage; and chestnut pastries filled with mushrooms. Reserve ahead. Cash only. (📞213 962 744; Rua da Esperança 112; small plates €8-12; ⏱7pm-2am Wed-Sat, 1.30pm-12.30am Sun)

A Travessa

PORTUGUESE €€€

16 🍴 Map p114, G3

This 17th-century convent cranks up the romance with its serene cloisters and brick vaulting. António Moita whets appetites with fresh wood-fired bread and wild mushrooms with scrambled eggs, followed by mains like venison medallions with truffles and crème brûlée with seasonal fruits. (📞213 902 034; www.atravessa.com; Travessa do Convento das Bernardas 12; mains €23-48; ⏱12.30-3.30pm & 8pm-midnight Tue-Fri, 8pm-midnight Mon & Sat)

Drinking

Le Chat

CAFE, BAR

17 🍷 Map p114, E4

Staring at the view of the docks and Ponte 25 de Abril is the prime activity on the terrace of this glass-walled cafe-bar. It's a casual spot for coffee by day or cocktails and mellow beats by night. Skip the food. (Jardim 9 de Abril; ⏱12.30pm-midnight Tue, Wed & Sun, 12.30pm-3am Thu-Sat)

A Paródia

BAR

18 🍷 Map p114, E1

This delightful bar time-warps you back to the more glamorous age of art nouveau, with its dark wood, red velvet walls, soft lamp lighting and vintage knick-knacks. It's a wonderfully cosy and intimate place for a tête-à-tête over cocktails, with jazz playing softly in the background. (Rua do Patrocínio 26; ⏱9pm-2am)

Matiz Pombalina

COCKTAIL BAR

19 🍷 Map p114, G3

Exposed stone walls, velvet sofas and soft lighting give this bar an intimate feel. Creative cocktails like Matiz (cold espresso, brandy and chocolate) are the big deal, and it also runs mixology workshops. (www.matiz-pombalina.pt; Rua das Trinas 25; ⏰7pm-2am Tue-Sat)

Foxtrot
BAR

20 🍺 Map p114, H1

A dark, decadent slither of art-nouveau glamour, Foxtrot keeps the mood mellow with jazzy beats, expertly mixed cocktails and enormous G&Ts. It's a wonderfully moody spot for a chat. (www.barfoxtrot.com; Travessa Santa Teresa 28; ⏰6pm-3am Mon-Sat, 8pm-2am Sun; 🛜)

K Urban Beach
CLUB

21 🍺 Map p114, G4

Jutting out over the Tejo, this stylish and airy club has a lively dance floor, a sushi restaurant and outdoor seating that makes fine use of its scenic riverside setting. (www.grupo-k.pt; Cais da Viscondessa, Santos; ⏰8pm-6am Tue-Sun)

Entertainment

Senhor Vinho
FADO

22 ⭐ Map p114, G2

Fado star Maria da Fé owns this small place, welcoming first-rate *fadistas*. Go for the fado not the food and feel free to refuse menu extras. (📞213 972 681; www.srvinho.com; Rua do Meio á Lapa; minimum €15; ⏰7.30pm-2am)

Shopping

Verso Branco
DESIGN

23 🔒 Map p114, H3

'Free verse' is the name of this split-level design store, where Fernando has a story for every object. The high-ceilinged space showcases Portuguese contemporary arts, crafts and furnishings, from Burel's quality wool creations to limited-edition La.Ga bags by designer Jorge Moita – the beautifully crafted bags made from Tyvek weigh just 40g and can hold 55kg. (Rua da Boavista 132-134; ⏰11.30am-8pm Tue-Sat)

Armazém Geral
ARTS & CRAFTS

24 🔒 Map p114, H2

Bruno, who runs We Hate Tourism Tours (p144), applies the same concept to this quirky general store and his HQ. 'Everything is made with amor' says the sign on the door and it's true – from knitwear to ceramics, notebooks to wine, this is perfect non-touristy gift-buying territory. (Rua Da Silva 27; ⏰11am-7pm Wed-Mon)

LX Market
MARKET

25 🔒 Map p114, B4

Vintage clothing, antiques, crafts, food and weird and wonderful plants – the LX Factory market is the place to find them. Live music keeps the Sunday shoppers entertained. (www.lxmarket.com.pt; Rua Rodrigues de Faria 103; ⏰11am-6pm Sun)

Effigy of Yellamma (Goddess of the Fallen) at Museu do Oriente (p116)

PAUL BERNHARDT/GETTY IMAGES ©

Ler Devagar BOOKS

Late-night bookworms and anyone who likes a good read will love this floor-to-ceiling temple of books at the LX Factory (see 25 🔓 Map p114, B4). Art, culture and foreign-language titles are well represented. (www.lerdevagar.com; Rua Rodrigues Faria 103; ⏱noon-9pm Mon, noon-midnight Tue-Thu, noon-2am Fri-Sat, 11am-9pm Sun)

Portugal Gifts GIFTS

26 🔓 Map p114, E4

This craft shop puts a contemporary spin on Portuguese souvenirs, with everything from funky Barcelos cockerel mugs to *azulejo* (tile) coffee coasters and chocolate sardines. (Rua Presidente Arriaga 60; ⏱10am-7pm Mon-Fri)

MO&TA Studio FASHION

To meet Portuguese designer Jorge Moita and see the full array of his La.Ga bags – which he affectionately calls his UFOs – visit his design workshop, at the same address as Frade dos Mares (see 12 ✕ Map p114, G3). You'll need to be buzzed in. The striking tear-shaped handbags made of superlightweight, incredibly resistant Tyvek bear the creatively unique hallmarks of female prisoners, designers and artists. (Ground floor, Avenida Dom Carlos I 55; ⏱9am-1pm & 2-5pm Mon-Fri)

Top Sights
Palácio Nacional de Sintra

Getting There

Sintra nestles among thickly wooded hills, 31km northwest of central Lisbon.

🚇 Train Trains run frequently from Rossio (€2.15, 40 minutes) and Oriente (€2.15, 50 minutes) stations.

The icing on Sintra's Unesco World Heritage cake, this sugar-white palace, crowned by a pair of huge conical chimneys, is pure fantasy stuff. Of Moorish origins, the palace was expanded by Dom Dinis (1261–1325), then enlarged by João I in the 15th century and given a Manueline makeover by Manuel I in the following century. Take in arabesque courtyards, barley-twist columns, and 15th- and 16th-century geometric *azulejos* (hand-painted tiles) – among Portugal's oldest – as you wander.

Don't Miss

Capela Palatina

This simple Moorish chapel, founded by Dom Dinis in the early 14th century, holds visitors captive with its mosaic of polychrome, geometric tiles, flock of frescoed doves and – above all – intricately carved, kaleidoscopic wood ceiling.

Sala dos Cisnes

Over the years, Portuguese royals have thrown banquets, court dances and festivals in this grand hall, its Renaissance-style gilded ceiling adorned with frescos of 27 gold-collared *cisnes* (swans).

Sala das Pegas

Suspicious? You will be looking up at the ceiling frieze of *pegas* (magpies). Lore has it that the queen caught João I kissing one of her ladies-in-waiting. The king professed innocence and commissioned one magpie for every lady-in-waiting to stop their tittle-tattle. Each holds a ribbon in its beak with the words *por bem* (in honour).

Palace Kitchen

Your gaze is drawn to the palace's iconic 33m-high chimneys in the kitchen. Built in the 15th century by João I, a king with an appetite for hunting, it was perfect for cooking the game to be served at royal banquets.

Sala dos Brasões

No surface is left unadorned in this chamber. Blue-and-white 18th-century *azulejos* depicting vivid hunting scenes guide the eye to an octagonal dome ceiling, which is emblazoned with the shields of 72 leading 16th-century families.

www.parquesdesintra.pt

Largo Rainha Dona Amélia

adult/child €9.50/7.50

9.30am-7pm, shorter hours in low season

☑ Top Tips

▸ Arrive early or late to avoid the biggest crowds.

▸ Make the most of free entry on Sunday mornings, until 2pm.

✗ Take a Break

Since 1756, **Fábrica das Verdadeiras Queijadas da Sapa** (Alameda Volta do Duche 12; 9am-6pm Tue-Fri, 9.30am-6.30pm Sat & Sun) has been rotting royal teeth with *queijadas*, pastry shells filled with a marzipan-like mix of fresh cheese, sugar, flour and cinnamon.

Since 1952, **Casa Piriquita** (Rua das Padarias 1-5; 9am-9pm Thu-Tue) has been tempting locals with another luscious sweet: the *travesseiro*, puff pastry filled with almond-and-egg-yolk cream.

The Best of
Lisbon

Torre de Belém (p126)
VICTOR ESTEVEZ/GETTY IMAGES ©

Best Walks
Belém's Age of Discovery

The Walk

A stroll through nautical-flavoured Belém, with its broad river views and exuberant Manueline architecture, catapults you back to Portugal's golden Age of Discovery – the 15th and 16th centuries, when explorers like Vasco da Gama and Henry the Navigator set sail for lands rich in gold and spices aboard mighty caravels, and Portugal was but a drop in King Manuel I's colonial ocean.

Start Praça do Império; 🚋15, 🚌28

Finish Torre de Belém; 🚌15, 🚌28

Length 2.5km; 1½ hours

Take a Break

Start or end your walk sweetly with a break at the Antiga Confeitaria de Belém (p85), a beautifully tiled patisserie that has been baking Lisbon's best *pastéis de Belém,* custard tarts served hot from the oven with a sprinkling of cinnamon, since 1837.

SYLVAIN SONNET/GETTY IMAGES ©

Mosteiro dos Jerónimos (p78)

❶ Praça do Império

Even blasé locals never tire of the uplifting view of the **Mosteiro dos Jerónimos** (p78) and Rio Tejo from this stately plaza, set around a fountain and fringed by box hedges. Note Age of Discovery symbols, such as anchors and the cross of the Military Order, featured in flowers and foliage.

❷ Maritime Map

Head across to the breezy riverfront promenade, looking down as you approach the Padrão dos Descobrimentos, to spot a **mosaic map** charting the routes of Portuguese mariners and the dates of colonisation, from the Azores (1427) to Calcutta (1498) and beyond.

❸ Padrão dos Descobrimentos

Like a caravel caught in mid-swell, the 52m-high **Padrão dos Descobrimentos** (p83) was inaugurated in 1960 on the 500th anniversary of Henry the Navigator's death. At the prow is Henry, while behind him are explorers Vasco da Gama, Diogo Cão, Fernão de Magalhães and 29 other greats.

❹ Doca do Bom Sucesso

Take a brisk walk along the riverfront to the Doca do Bom Sucesso, where you can watch the boats and seagulls over drinks at waterfront **Bar 38° 41'** (p87). This is a relaxed spot to dip into Luís Vaz de Camões' *The Lusiads,*

an epic poem recounting Vasco da Gama's explorations.

❺ Torre de Belém

Feel the pull of the past and the breezes of the Atlantic as you gaze up at the **Torre de Belém** (p83), an early 16th-century icon of the Age of Discovery and a prime example of whimsical Manueline style with its ribbed cupolas.

❻ Hidden Rhino

It's easy to miss one of the Torre de Belém's most intriguing features. Below the western tower is a **rhinoceros**, a stone carving of the Indian rhino Manuel I shipped to Pope Leo X as a token of his esteem in 1515. The rhino never reached Rome – it drowned when the ship capsized – but Albrecht Dürer immortalised it in his famous woodcut.

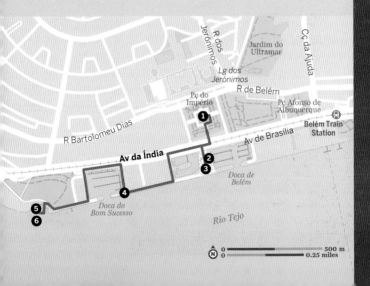

Best Walks
Baixa to Santa Catarina

🏃 The Walk

Shopping in Baixa's old-world stores, culture in Chiado's museums, captivating sunset views from Santa Catarina – it's all packed into this 'greatest hits' tour of downtown Lisbon. This afternoon walk gives you a palpable sense of Lisbon's history – on Baixa's regal plazas, in Pombaline backstreets built in the wake of the 1755 earthquake, and in literary-flavoured cafes, where poets like Fernando Pessoa once hung out.

Start Praça do Comércio; Ⓜ Terreiro do Paço

Finish Santa Catarina; 🚋28

Length 4.5km; 3½ hours

✕ Take a Break

Enjoy coffee and cake on the terrace of Confeitaria Nacional (p45). Across the way from the Casa do Ferreira das Tabuletas, the Royale Café (p25) has a vine-clad courtyard for a relaxed lunch.

Praça da Figueira (p49)

❶ Praça do Comércio

At Lisbon's riverside gateway, **Praça do Comércio** (p42), trams rumble past palatial facades, arcades and a gallant equestrian statue of Dom José I. Nip into **ViniPortugal** (p43) to taste Portuguese wines for €2.

❷ Rua Augusta

Pass through the triumphal **Arco da Vitória** (p43) onto the main thoroughfare, Rua Augusta, buzzing with street entertainers and shoppers. From here, explore backstreets like old-fashioned **Rua da Conceição** (p45).

❸ Elevador de Santa Justa

When you hit Rua de Santa Justa, swing left for the neo-Gothic **Elevador de Santa Justa** (p47), Lisbon's only vertical street lift. Enjoy 360-degree views from the viewing platform.

❹ Praça da Figueira

Saunter east along Rua de Santa Justa then north up Rua da Prata to **Praça da Figueira** (p49) for castle views from below. The square is rimmed with cafes and old-school stores.

❺ Rossio

Head straight onto **Rossio** (p47), one of Lisbon's grandest squares with its wave-like cobbles, fountains, neoclassical theatre and neo-Manueline **Estação do Rossio** (p47).

❻ Largo do Carmo

Behind the train station, Calçada do Carmo climbs to Chiado's **Largo do Carmo**, where jacaranda trees shade pavement cafes and the 18th-century Chafariz do Carmo fountain. Rising above it are the ethereal arches of the ruined **Convento do Carmo** (p24).

❼ Casa do Ferreira das Tabuletas

Cross the square to Rua da Trindade and the 1864 **Casa do Ferreira das Tabuletas**, where the *trompe l'œil azulejos* (hand-painted tiles) depict allegorical figures and the elements.

❽ Rua Serpa Pinto

Follow the road south, past the 18th-century opera house **Teatro Nacional de São Carlos** (p35). Further on is modern art gallery **Museu do Chiado** (p30).

❾ Santa Catarina

Turn right and follow the trams along elegant Rua de São Paulo for a ride on the 1892 **Elevador da Bica** (p31). Descend Rua Marechal Saldanha to **Miradouro de Santa Catarina** (p31) for sunset views of the river.

Best
Food

HEMIS/ALAMY ©

While classics like *bacalhau* (dried salt-cod) and *pastéis de nata* (custard tarts) never go out of fashion, the Portuguese capital has raised the culinary bar recently, with creative, open-minded chefs looking towards Brazil, France, India and the Med for inspiration. Individualism trumps conformity and restaurants are popping up in the most unlikely places, from convents to pharmaceutical museums and former fish-tackle stores.

Tasca Charm

Crowded tables, an inviting buzz and trusted menus with robust Portuguese dishes like *açorda* (bread and shellfish stew) define *tascas*, Lisbon's family-run, cheap-as-chips eateries. Some of the best are tucked away in the backstreets of Baixa, Alfama and Bairro Alto. Find an equally local scene and great-value specials at *churrasqueiras* (grill houses).

Fine Dining

Simplicity, pristine ingredients and creativity mark Lisbon's gourmet scene. Chefs such as José Avillez (Belcanto; p33), João Rodrigues (Feitoria; p86) and Vitor Areias (Assinatura; p106) have put the Portuguese capital on the gastro map with ingredient-focused tasting menus, often putting a spin on comfort foods like slow-cooked suckling pig and *bacalhau*.

Cookery Classes

If you're into Portuguese food in a big way and fancy picking up a few tips and tricks from the experts, why not pass by **Kiss the Cook** (www.kissthecook.pt) at the LX Factory (p117) in Alcântara? Here you can prepare (and devour) traditional dishes. The cookery classes are totally hands-on and the €65 price tag includes lunch and wine. Book ahead.

☑ Top Tips

▶ You can eat well for very little in Lisbon, especially if you opt for the good-value *menu do dia* (fixed menu) or *prato do dia* (daily special). Lunch is an inexpensive way to dine at even the best restaurants.

▶ *Couvert*, the bread, olives and other goodies automatically brought to the table as appetisers, costs. You pay for what you eat, but it's fine to send it away if you don't want it.

Pharmacia (p32)

Best Bistros

Frade dos Mares Slick, modern bistro with spot-on grilled meats and fish. (p118)

Le Petit Bistro Retro-chic bistro in the Bica area, with a French and global menu. (p32)

Santa Clara dos Cogumelos A slice of vintage cool in a former market hall, with a mushroom-focused menu. (p68)

Clube das Jornalistas Pared-down elegance in an 18th-century house opening onto a tree-shaded courtyard. (p118)

Best Gourmet

Belcanto Could José Avillez' two-Michelin-star halo shine any brighter? Art on a plate. (p33)

Feitoria João Rodrigues elevates seasonal ingredients to a whole new level at this riverfront gourmet haunt in Belém. (p86)

Assinatura Tucked-away gourmet haunt where chef Vitor Areias puts a modern spin on Portuguese cuisine. (p106)

Best for Romance

100 Maneiras Intimate Bairro Alto bistro made for lingering over the well-executed 10-course menu. (p33)

Casa da Comida Romance is a palm-shaded courtyard, an antique-studded interior and food cooked with passion and precision. (p106)

A Travessa Beautifully cooked Portuguese specialties served around the cloister of a 17th-century monastery. (p119)

Best Tapas

Fumeiro de Santa Catarina New-wave *petiscos* (tapas) in a retro-cool setting. (p31)

Grapes & Bites Snug Bairro Alto wine bar with great tipples, tapas and a buzz. (p31)

Bebedouro Hip 'n' happening wine and tapas bar in Baixa with pavement seating. (p51)

Pharmacia Appetising tapas and pharmaceutical fun in Lisbon's apothecary museum. (p32)

Best
Shopping

In the age of the one-size-fits-all mall, shopping in Lisbon is a breath of fresh air. Trawl the elegant streets of Baixa and Chiado for a taste of the good old days in art-deco shops dealing solely in perfume or buttons, tinned fish or custom-made gloves. Go to Bairro Alto for vintage chic and urban streetwear, Estrela for antiques and art, Príncipe Real for forward-thinking design.

GREG ELMS/GETTY IMAGES ©

Best Food

Conserveira de Lisboa A 1930s time warp selling every tinned fish imaginable, all packaged in retro paper. (p45)

Manuel Tavares Doing a brisk trade in cheese, chocolate, port and other Portuguese treats since 1860. (p45)

Napoleão A welcoming shop for Portuguese wine, port, Madeira and *ginjinha* (cherry liqueur). (p54)

Queijaria Nacional Superb cheese shop with varieties from the Alentejo to the Azores. (p54)

Best Fashion & Vintage

Outra Face da Lua Looking for a '60s shirt or a vintage prom dress? You'll find it here. (p45)

Story Tailors A wonderland of floaty, fairy-tale couture by Lisbon duo Luís and João. (p37)

Kolovrat 79 The flagship store of Lisbon's daring darling of fashion, Lidija Kolovrat. (p39)

Best Speciality Shops

A Vida Portuguesa Emporium of old-fashioned Portuguese goods: from Tricana sardines to prettily wrapped Claus Porto soaps. (p36)

Luvaria Ulisses Find a glove that fits in beautifully soft leather at this shoebox-sized 1920s shop. (p37)

Cortiço & Netos A retro wonderland of industrial *azulejos*, run with passion by three brothers. (p72)

Best Art & Design

Embaixada A 19th-century neo-Moorish palace turned mini-mall, with fashion, design and concept stores. (p39)

Verso Branco Contemporary Portuguese arts and crafts are in the spotlight at this split-level store. (p120)

Best Markets

Feira da Ladra Hunt for treasures at this vibrant flea market on Campo de Santa Clara. (p72)

Mercado da Ribeira Riverside market hall dating to 1882 with Time Out gourmet food court. (p37)

LX Market Popular Sunday market at the LX Factory, with everything from food to vintage clothing. (p120)

Best
Bars & Nightlife

As one local put it, Lisbon is Europe's Havana, with its decadence, bright-coloured buildings and party-loving vibe. And whether you're toasting new-found friendships in Bairro Alto's narrow lanes, rocking to live gigs in Cais do Sodré or sipping *ginjinha* (cherry liquer) around Rossio at dusk, you can't help but be swept along by the festive spirit in this most sociable of cities.

PAUL BERNHARDT/GETTY IMAGES ©

Nightlife Districts

Take the lead of locals and begin an evening in front of a cubby-hole *ginjinha* bar around Rossio. In the mood for fado? Gravitate towards the medina-like Alfama for the real deal in softly lit, family-run clubs. Bairro Alto is one big street party and bar-hopping after midnight is the way to go. Similarly open-minded, bohemian and oblivious to sleep is sleazy-turned-trendy Cais do Sodré, with a growing crop of bordello-chic bars and all-night clubs. For a more low-key, gay-friendly vibe in cocktail bars and en-vogue cafes, swing north to Príncipe Real. Edging west of the centre, industrial-cool bars and clubs draw crowds to the riverside in Alcântara.

Best Bars

Cinco Lounge Beetroot margarita anyone? Dave is the mixology master at this slick Príncipe Real bar. (p39)

Pensão Amor Brothel turned staggeringly popular bar and arts centre. (p27)

A Ginjinha Hands-down our favourite spot for a sundown tipple of *ginjinha*. (pictured above; p52)

Park Multi-storey car park turned hip rooftop bar, with expansive views and DJs. (p34)

Best Live Music

Music Box Emerging bands perform at this happening haunt under the bridge. (p27)

Povo Fado pure, simple and unplugged, with a different *fadista* in residence every month. (p27)

Fado in Chiado Hour-long evening fado show held in the heart of Chiado. (p36)

Best Clubs

Lux-Frágil John Malkovich's clubbing temple: great DJs, river views, friendly vibe. (p70)

Clube Ferroviário All aboard the night train at this railway-themed lounge and club in Santa Apolónia. (p69)

Best
Museums & Galleries

If Lisbon's museums and galleries have side-stepped the world spotlight, it's because the Portuguese capital whispers about its charms. Yet it has been hoarding fine art for centuries. You'll find Rodin sculptures and works by Dutch Masters, Dürer and Warhol in its uncrowded galleries, while museums showcasing royal carriages, fado memorabilia and geometric *azulejos* zoom in on Portugal's rich heritage and history.

JOHN HARPER/GETTY IMAGES ©

☑ Top Tips

▶ Many museums offer free entry on Sundays (usually to 2pm).

▶ For more savings on museum entry, invest in a Lisboa Card (p149).

Best Ancient & Decorative Arts

Museu Calouste Gulbenkian Treasure-trove museum with standout Egyptian artefacts, Rubens paintings and René Lalique jewellery. (p100)

Museu Nacional de Arte Antiga Peerless stash of ancient art, from Dürer originals to bejewelled chalices and Japanese screens. (p112)

Museu de Artes Decorativas Qing porcelain and French silverware in a petite 17th-century palace. (p66)

Casa-Museu Medeiros e Almeida An unsung gem of a private collection in an art-nouveau mansion. (p104)

Best Modern & Contemporary Art

Museu Colecção Berardo Warhol pop art and Picasso cubist wonders crown this outstanding collection. (p80)

Centro de Arte Moderna Homing in on 20th- and 21st-century art, with works by Hockney, Gormley and Paula Rego. (p104)

Museu do Chiado Beautifully converted convent with star pieces by Rodin and Jorge Vieira. (p30)

Best for Heritage

Museu Nacional do Azulejo Piece together 500 years of *azulejo* history. (p75)

Museu Nacional dos Coches A fantasy of fairy-tale coaches in the former royal riding stables. (p83)

Museu de Marinha Circumnavigate the Age of Discovery studying cannonballs and shipwreck treasures. (pictured above; p83)

Museu do Oriente Be catapulted back to Portugal's first baby steps in Asia. (p116)

Museu do Fado Tune into the history of fado at this folk-music museum. (p66)

Best
Azulejos

CHIARA SALVADOR/GETTY IMAGES ©

Plain and patterned, ornamental and utilitarian, blue-and-white and polychrome – *azulejos* adorn facades all over Lisbon. The Moors introduced these glazed ceramic tiles to Portugal in the 15th century, taking their name from the Arabic word *zellij* (polished stone). Now they are everywhere you look, adding a touch of art to the everyday.

Art Underground

Some of Lisbon's finest *azulejos* can't be seen at street level. Maria Keil kick-started a new form of underground art when she let her imagination loose on metro stations in 1957, ultimately decorating 19 of them with her geometric and abstract designs. Today, for the price of a ticket, you can take in an *azulejo* zoo of animals at Jardim Zoológico, quench your thirst looking at Sá Nogueira's juicy oranges at Laranjeiras (literally 'orange trees') and be swept back to the Age of Discovery in maritime-themed Parque. Spot philosophers and owls at Cidade Universitária, the White Rabbit from *Alice in Wonderland* at Cais do Sodré and poet Fernando Pessoa at Alto dos Moinhos. Arguably the fairest *azulejos* of all are at Gare do Oriente.

Best Church Azulejos

Igreja & Museu São Roque Extraordinary diamond-tip majolica tiles grace this unassuming church. (p30)

Igreja de São Vicente de Fora See La Fontaine fables picked out in *azulejos* and an exquisitely tiled cloister. (p66)

Best Ornamental Azulejos

Museu Nacional do Azulejo An ode to the *azulejo* in every style, shape and form. (p75)

Palácio Nacional de Sintra Sintra's fairy-tale palace has *azulejos* from almost every epoch. (pictured above; p122)

Mosteiro dos Jerónimos Belém's Manueline monastery hides fine examples of 18th-century *azulejo* friezes. (p78)

Best Take-Home Azulejos

Fábrica Sant'Ana Hand-making and -painting *azulejos* using age-old techniques since 1741. (p37)

Loja dos Descobrimentos Watch artisans at work and buy *azulejos* of your own. (p73)

Cortiço & Netos Industrial tiles elevated to an art form at this born-again family business. (p72)

Best
Contemporary Art & Design

FORGET GAUTIER/AGE FOTOSTOCK ©

Though often seen as more traditional than trendsetting, Lisbon has quietly but confidently been evolving as a centre of urban art and contemporary design. Finally, it is ready to be feted. From Picoas' larger-than-life graffiti murals to Príncipe Real's interior design stores, Bairro Alto's newly minted galleries and industrial-minimalist art spaces in Alcântara, the Portuguese capital is crackling with creativity.

Urban Art

Street art is changing the face of Lisbon's derelict apartment blocks, thanks to the **Crono Project** (www.cargocollective.com/crono), an initiative to spruce up the capital together with 16 of Europe's top urban artists. Top of your street-art itinerary should be the graffiti works splashed across facades near Picoas metro station. On Avenida Fontes Pereira de Melo, you can't miss SAM3's giant shadow set against a night sky and Blu's crown-wearing bigwig sucking the world dry. On the corner of Rua Martens Ferrão, keep an eye out for Ericailcane's crocodile and Lucy McLauchlan's graphic bird murals. Among the other highlights is Boris Hoppek's *Mudhead* in Alcântara and Italian artist Momo's abstract, rainbow-bright mural on Avenida Almirante Reis.

Best Contemporary Art

Centro de Arte Moderna Gallery of 20th- and 21st-century art, from Antony Gormley to Paula Rego. (p104)

Museu Colecção Berardo Outstanding collection: Warhol, Hockney, Lichtenstein, Man Ray, Miró and more. (p80)

Parque das Nações Street Art Find open-air art along the riverside promenade, from Jorge Vieira to Antony Gormley sculptures (p94).

Best Design

LX Factory A 19th-century textile factory turned arts centre, home to design studios, galleries and workshops. (p117)

Museu de Design e da Moda A fascinating (free) romp into 20th- and 21st-century design. (pictured above; p49)

PAUL BERNHARDT/GETTY IMAGES ©

♥ Best
Pastelarias & Cafes

Sweet tooth? One visit to Lisbon's *pastelarias* (pastry shops) and you'll be hooked, we swear. Perhaps by the *pastéis de nata* (caramelised custard tarts that crumble just so); perhaps by the sumptuous gilt and stucco surrounds of old-world cafes; perhaps by the new-generation bakeries doing a brisk trade in French patisserie and cupcakes that are (almost) too pretty to eat.

Best Old-School Pastelarias

Antiga Confeitaria de Belém Lisbon's best *pastéis de nata* since 1837. (pictured above; p85)

Versailles Rather grand 1930s patisserie frequented for cream cakes and gossip. (p105)

Pastelaria São Roque Prettily tiled patisserie for buttery rock cakes and freshly baked bread. (p32)

Best Sweet Temptations

Tease A mosaic of *azulejos* gives a touch of decadence to this cupcake wonderland in Príncipe Real. (p39)

Fábrica das Verdadeiras Queijadas da Sapa Famous for its *queijadas* (cheesecakes) since 1756. One delicious bite and they're gone. (p123)

Landeau Divine chocolate cake. Enough said. (p118)

Manteigaria Born-again butter factory with *pastéis de nata* (pictured above) to blow you away. (p32)

Best Cafes with a View

Lost In A taste of India and captivating castle views await at this well-hidden, colour-charged cafe. (p33)

Le Chat This glass-fronted cafe has fine views of the Alcântara docks. (p119)

Noobai Café Santa Catarina cafe with a tucked-away terrace for sundowners and twilight city views. (p34)

Best Relaxed Cafes

Pois Café This boho cafe has a laid-back vibe, creative salads and sandwiches. (p68)

Cruzes Credo Café Close to the cathedral, this atmospheric cafe combines a brick-vaulted interior with a pocket-sized terrace. (p69)

Esplanada Birdsong, people-watching and a giant cedar tree for a parasol. (p39)

Fábulas A fantasy fairy tale of a cafe, with a mellow vibe and appetising light bites. (p33)

Best
Viewpoints

Like Rome, Lisbon sits astride seven hills, which equates to a different view for every day of the week. You might huff and puff and curse this hilly town as you climb the umpteenth cobbled *calçada* (stairway), but take heart: for every stairway there is a beguiling *miradouro* (viewpoint), for every blister a(nother) breathtaking vista.

MARK AVELLINO/GETTY IMAGES ©

Best Bairro Miradouros

Miradouro de São Pedro de Alcântara This tree-shaded, fountain-dotted terrace has far-reaching views to the castle, the river and the Ponte 25 de Abril. (p30)

Miradouro de Santa Catarina Buskers, artists, families, couples – everyone loves the river views from Santa Catarina, especially at sundown. (p31)

Best Alfama & Graça Miradouros

Largo das Portas do Sol Peer across Alfama's mosaic of red rooftops, spires and domes to the Rio Tejo at this Moorish gateway. (p63)

Miradouro de Santa Luzia Prettily tiled terrace draped with bougainvillea

and commanding long views across Alfama and Baixa. (p62)

Miradouro da Senhora do Monte They don't come higher than this pine-shaded viewpoint, affording photogenic perspectives of the castle. (p63)

Miradouro da Graça Popular sunset gathering spot with amazing views of Lisbon's skyline. (p63)

Best Bars with Views

Memmo Alfama A magic trick of a rooftop bar, buried deep in the medieval heart of Alfama. (p69)

Noobai Café A perfect sunset spot, this terrace has cracking views of the Tejo and Ponte 25 de Abril. (p34)

☑ **Top Tips**

▶ Want to linger? Most of the *miradouros* (viewpoints) have kiosk cafes where you can grab a drink and snack.

▶ Don't just visit by day: evenings, when the city is aglow, can be just as atmospheric, if not more.

Bairro Alto Hotel Chic lounge terrace for cocktail imbibing as Lisbon lights up. (p34)

Sky Bar Lisbon opens out like a pop-up book before you from the Tivoli's sophisticated terrace. (p108)

Rooftop Bar Slinky white sofas, cool drinks, jazzy beats and prime views of the castle on the hillside. (p52)

Best
Outdoors

While Lisbon might not immediately strike you as a green city, there are well-tended parks, botanical gardens lush with palms and banyan trees, and fountain-dotted *praças* (squares) offering peaceful respite if you know where to look. For refreshing Atlantic breezes on a summer's day, head to the riverfront where you can stroll, cycle and tick off some of the city's landmarks.

Beside the Sea

Bet you didn't think you'd need your bucket and spade for a trip to Lisbon. Yet the coast is incredibly close. Board a train at Cais do Sodré and within 40 minutes you can be paddling in the Atlantic, licking ice cream and eating just-caught fish in Cascais. Take your pick of its bays or hire a bike (free) from the station to pedal along the coast to the villa-studded resort of Estoril, the 19th-century seaside playground of the rich and famous. Want to catch some waves? Praia do Guincho, 9km northwest of Cascais, attracts surfers, kitesurfers and windsurfers to its wave-lashed beach.

Best Parks & Promenades

Jardim da Estrela Wander among the palms, pines and monkey-puzzle trees. A playground and duck ponds appeal to kids. (p116)

Parque Eduardo VII Gaze across Lisbon to the river from the top of this sloping parterre. (p104)

Ribeira das Naus A gorgeous promenade lopes along Lisbon's revamped riverfront. (p50)

Best Botanical Gardens

Jardim Garcia de Orta A riverside park nurturing colonial flora from dragon trees to frangipani. (p93)

Jardim Botânico Madeiran geraniums, jacarandas and a giant Moreton Bay fig tree thrive in this pocket of greenery north of Bairro Alto. (p105)

Estufas Take a botanical stroll around this trio of glasshouses, harbouring camellias and coffee and mango trees. (p104)

Best Squares

Praça do Comércio Down by the river, this monumental square is the Lisbon of a million postcards. (pictured above; p42)

Rossio Wavelike cobbles, fountains, cafes and a 24-hour buzz. (p47)

Praça do Príncipe Real A giant umbrella of a Mexican cedar shades this plaza, with a kids playground and open-air cafe. (p39)

THOMAS PETER WIDMANN/LOOK-FOTO/GETTY IMAGES ©

Best
For Kids

Keeping the kids amused in Lisbon is child's play. Even the everyday can be incredibly exciting: custard tarts for breakfast, rickety rides on vintage trams and Willy Wonka–like funiculars. Then there is the castle straight from the pages of a story book, swashbuckling tales of great navigators in Belém, riverside parks and nearby beaches for free play. As cities go, this is kid heaven.

PAUL BERNHARDT/GETTY IMAGES ©

Kids in Tow

Travelling with a family can quickly add up, but Lisbon has some excellent deals for those in the know. Many museums and sights offer free entry for under-12s or under-14s, while those under 18 get a 50% discount. Hotels are usually well geared to families and many will squeeze in a cot at no extra charge. We're not going to deny it: the cobblestones make pushchairs hard work, but getting around on public transport is a breeze and under-fours travel free. Kids are welcome in nearly all restaurants and *meia dose* (small portions) are ideal for little appetites.

Best Hands-On Fun

Oceanário Sharks, sea otters and weird and wonderful fish splash around at Europe's second-largest aquarium. (p90)

Pavilhão do Conhecimento Physics is (finally) a bundle of laughs at this hands-on science centre. (pictured above; p93)

Castelo de São Jorge A whopper of a castle with ramparts for exploring and a hair-raising history. (p60)

Best Museums

Museu de Marinha Kids can embark on their own voyage of discovery at this barge-stuffed museum. (p83)

Museu Nacional dos Coches Royal coaches that are pure Cinderella stuff. (p83)

Museu da Marioneta Kids love the worldly puppets at this Geppetto's workshop of a museum. (p117)

Best Outdoors

Jardim Botânico Tropical Cool off with your kids in the shade of these botanical gardens in Belém, home to sprawling banyan trees and friendly ducks. (p85)

Jardins d'Água The splashy fun is endless at these water gardens in Parque das Nações. (p95)

Jardim da Estrela Low-key park with duck ponds and an animal-themed playground. (p116)

Best
Tram & Funicular Rides

Vintage trams are to Lisbon what the red double-decker is to London and the gondola to Venice. Much more than a way of getting from A to B, these rides are whistle-stop city tours and a flashback to late-19th-century life. Century-old funiculars breeze up Lisbon's hills, emerging within minutes at viewpoints where the entire city spreads out photogenically before you.

VISIONS OF OUR LAND/GETTY IMAGES ©

Lisbon's Trams

Planning a trip on tram 28? Begin where the tram starts on Largo Martim Moniz to stand a chance of getting a seat in the wood-panelled carriage. Among the city's other attractive, lesser-known tram rides are the circular route from Praça da Figueira, taking in Alfama views from Largo das Portas do Sol and Sé (cathedral); tram 18 from Rua Alfândega to the Palácio da Ajuda via Alcântara; and tram 15 from Praça da Figueira, which trundles along the riverfront to Belém. A day travel pass (€6), which you can purchase from metro stations, gives you the freedom to hop on and off as you please and covers all trams and funiculars.

Best Tram Ride

Tram 28 Lisbon's old-time tram rattles past some of the city's most iconic landmarks – from Sé to the Basílica da Estrela. (p56)

Elevador da Bica Enjoy snapshot views of the river on the steep ascent of Rua da Bica de Duarte Belo aboard this 1892 funicular. (p31)

Elevador da Glória This funicular has been clanking uphill from Praça dos Restauradores to Miradouro São Pedro de Alcântara since 1885. (p30)

Best Funiculars

Elevador de Santa Justa Ride this neo-Gothic wonder, designed by Eiffel's protégé, for 360-degree city views. (pictured above; p47)

Best
Churches, Castles & Palaces

The Moors and Christian crusaders, fairy-tale-minded King Manuel I and one hell of an earthquake in 1755 have all left their indelible mark on Lisbon. Exploring the city you will be confronted with a rich tapestry of history, which pieces seamlessly together as you wander castle ramparts and cloisters, *azulejo*-filled baroque churches and palaces straight out of a story book.

ARPAD BENEDEK/GETTY IMAGES ©

Best Palaces & Castles

Palácio Nacional de Sintra Conical chimneys crown this palace, hiding Moorish courtyards, Manueline flourishes and a fantasy of *azulejos*. (p123)

Castelo de São Jorge Perkily set on a hillside, Lisbon's crowning-glory castle tells its history in a nutshell. Get wide-angle views of the city from the ramparts. (p60)

Best Churches & Cathedrals

Igreja Santa Maria de Belém A spiderweb of stone canopies this enchanting Manueline church, where great navigator Vasco da Gama lies buried. (p79)

Sé Gargoyles keep watch at this Gothic giant of a cathedral, built on the site of a mosque in 1150. (p66)

Basílica da Estrela Dona Maria I commissioned this domed neoclassical basilica to celebrate the birth of a male heir. It was completed in 1790. (p116)

Igreja de São Roque Behind a nondescript facade, this 16th-century Jesuit church is a jewel box of gold, marble, lapis lazuli and Florentine *azulejos*. (pictured above; p30)

Igreja de São Domingos The Portuguese Inquisition, the 1755 earthquake, raging fire – this enigmatic church bears the scars of its dark past. (p49)

Igreja de São Vicente de Fora Part of a monastery, this twin-towered Renaissance church shelters royal tombs. (p66)

Best
Free Lisbon

Clichéd though it sounds, the best things in Lisbon really are free. *Miradouros* with fabulous views? Free. Lisbon's *azulejo*-lined stations, riverside promenades and monumental squares? Free. Backstreet strolls in the Moorish Alfama? You guessed it: free. Even contemporary art, Roman ruins, wine tasting and cutting-edge design can be enjoyed without dishing out the euros in this already remarkably good value city.

HOLGER LEUE/GETTY IMAGES ©

Sightseeing Savers

With a little careful planning, you can whittle down sightseeing costs considerably. Why not swap that city tour for your own self-guided one on vintage tram 28, where you can tick off the major landmarks for the price of a ticket? Or save Lisbon sightseeing for Sunday mornings when it costs nothing to visit the big-hitter museums and sights, including the Mosteiro dos Jerónimos, Museu Calouste Gulbenkian, Museu Nacional de Arte Antiga and Museu Nacional do Azulejo.

Best Free Art

Museu Colecção Berardo A rocket ride through modern and contemporary art – Warhol, Miró, Lichtenstein, you name it. (p80)

Museu de Design e da Moda Trace the evolution of design from the 1930s to the present. (p49)

Best Free Sights

Museu do Teatro Romano A ruined theatre

spells out Lisbon's Roman past in stone. (p67)

Sé A Gothic giant of a cathedral, lit by a beautiful rose window. (p66)

Núcleo Arqueológico Find buried treasures on a free guided tour of these archaeological remains. (p49)

Basílica da Estrela Topped by an ivory-white dome, this basilica has amazing grace. (pictured above; p116)

☑ Top Tips

▶ For the inside scoop on the city, **Sandemans** (www.newlisbontours.com) fun, informative and free three-hour walking tours of downtown Lisbon are hard to beat. You'll do the rounds of all the major landmarks and get versed in history as you stroll. Tours begin at 11am daily at the monument on Praça Luís de Camões.

▶ On the first Sunday of the month, catch the free recital in the foyer of the Museu Calouste Gulbenkian.

Best
Tours

Best Bus & Boat Tours

Transtejo (☎210 422 417; www.transtejo.pt; Terreiro do Paço ferry terminal; adult/child €20/10; ☺Apr-Oct) A relaxed way to see the city from the river, these 2½-hour boat tours depart from Terreiro do Paço, passing landmarks like the Ponte 25 de Abril and the ship-shaped Padrão dos Descobrimentos.

Yellow Bus Tours (www.yellowbustours.com; adult/child €15/7.50; ☺departures every 15 mins 9am-8pm) Tram 28 covers the major sights, but if you'd prefer to join a group, Yellow Bus Tours runs two-hour open-top bus tours of city highlights, departing from Praça Figueira.

Best Walking & Bike Tours

Lisbon Explorer (☎213 629 263; www.lisbonexplorer.com; adult/child €35/free) English-speaking guides peel back the many layers of Lisbon's history during these highly rated three-hour walking tours. 'Hidden Lisbon' delves into Baixa, Chiado and Bairro Alto.

Lisbon Spirit (☎911 786 954; www.lisbon-spirit.pt; adult/child €15/free) These 3½-hour walking tours give brilliant insight into Lisbon, each covering one neighbourhood (Baixa, Belém, Bairro Alto etc). Their tour to the other side of the river affords different city perspectives.

Lisbon Bike Tour (☎912 272 300; www.lisbonbiketour.com; adult/child €29/15; ☺9.30am-1pm) It's all downhill on this 3½-hour guided bike ride from Marquês de Pombal to Belém.

HOLGER LEUE/GETTY IMAGES ©

Best Unusual Tours

We Hate Tourism Tours (☎913 776 598; www.wehatetourismtours.com; Rua da Silva 27; per person €15-60) One memorable way to explore the city is with Bruno, who takes travellers around in his iconic open-topped UMM (a Portuguese 4WD once made for the army). Besides his 'King of the Hills' tour, he leads night-life tours, beach trips and excursions to Sintra.

Go Car Tours (☎210 965 030; www.gocartours.pt; Rua dos Douradores 16; per hr/day €29/89; ☺9.30am-6.30pm) These self-guided tours put you behind the wheel of an open-topped two-seater mini-car with a talking GPS that guides you along one of several pre-determined routes. Helmets included.

Survival Guide

Survival Guide

Before You Go

When to Go

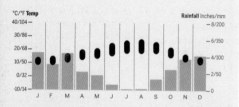

°C/°F Temp
40/104 —
30/86 —
20/68 —
10/50 —
0/32 —
-10/14 —

Rainfall Inches/mm
— 8/200
— 6/150
— 4/100
— 2/50
— 0

J F M A M J J A S O N D

➡ **Winter (Nov–Feb)**
Quiet except for Carnival in February. Low-season deals available. Weather can be wet and windy.

➡ **Spring (Mar–May)**
Parks in bloom, mild and often sunny days, accommodation still reasonably priced – perfect season for exploring.

➡ **Summer (Jun–Aug)**
Usually hot. Best time for open-air festivals, beach days and alfresco dining. Rooms are at a premium; book ahead.

➡ **Autumn (Sep–Oct)**
Pleasant temps, culture-focused events and few crowds, though spontaneous showers are to be expected.

Book Your Stay

➡ Book ahead during the high season (mid-July to mid-September).

➡ If you arrive without a reservation, head to a tourist office, where staff can call around for you.

➡ Many guesthouses lack lifts, meaning you'll have to haul your luggage up three flights or more. If this disconcerts, be sure to book a place with a lift.

➡ *Pensões* and *residenciais* are small-scale guesthouses, often with a personal feel. The best are generally better than the cheapest hotels. Rates usually include breakfast.

➡ Hotels normally drop prices in low season.

➡ Short-stay apartments are an alternative to hotels.

Useful Websites

Lonely Planet (www.lonelyplanet.com/hotels) Our pick of Lisbon's best accommodation.

Go Lisbon (www.golisbon.com/hotels) Book central apartments or search for hotels.

Lisbon 30 (www.lisbon30.com) Good-value hotels, hostels, apartments and B&Bs.

Rent 4 Days (www.rent-4days.com) Self-catering digs: from luxury flats to loft conversions.

Traveling to Lisbon (www.travelingtolisbon.com) Apartment rentals in and around Lisbon.

Best Budget

Travellers House (www.travellershouse.com) Funky, good-value option in the heart of Baixa.

Lisbon Destination Hostel (www.destinationhostels.com) Skylit, laid-back hostel in Rossio train station.

This is Lisbon (www.thisislisbonhostel.com) Great views and an easygoing vibe at this Brazilian-run hilltop perch in Castelo.

Living Lounge (www.livingloungehostel.com) Stylish, friendly hostel right in the heart of the action.

Lisbon Lounge Hostel (www.lisbonlounge-hostel.

com) Nicely chilled Baixa digs, with artfully designed dorms.

Alfama Patio Hostel (http://alfama.destinationhostels.com) Chilled Alfama hostel, with loads of activities, a stylish lounge and a relaxed garden patio.

Best Midrange

Casa Amora (www.casaamora.com) Beautifully designed guesthouse in Amoreiras, with eye-catching art and a lovely garden patio.

Casa do Bairro (www.shiadu.com) Small welcoming guesthouse, with bright rooms in contemporary style.

Lisbon Story Guesthouse (www.lisbonstoryguesthouse.com) Overlooking Largo de São Domingos, this small, welcoming guesthouse has light-drenched rooms with Portuguese themes.

Lisbon Dreams (www.lisbondreamsguesthouse.com) Tasteful high-ceilinged rooms and chilled-out courtyards.

Casa de São Mamede (www.casadesaomamede.com) Near the botanical gardens, this 18th-century,

family-run villa has rooms with period furnishings.

Hotel Eurostars das Letras (www.eurostarsdasletras.com) This handsomely designed hotel's high-tech rooms have a literary theme.

Best Top End

Chiado 16 (www.chiado16.com) Chiado boutique charmer, with just seven rooms – some with panoramic views.

Memmo Alfama (www.memmoalfama.com) Boutique newcomer in Alfama's medieval heart, with a stunning river-view roof terrace.

Hotel Britania (www.heritage.pt) Art-deco boutique gem near Avenida da Liberdade.

Lapa Palace (www.lapapalace.com) Exquisite 19th-century palace set in landscaped gardens.

As Janelas Verdes (www.heritage.pt) Romantic 18th-century mansion; bougainvillea-draped courtyard.

Altis Belém (www.altishotels.com) Hypermodern boutique hotel and spa near the waterfront in Belém.

Arriving in Lisbon

From Lisbon Airport

☑ **Top Tip** For the best way to reach your accommodation, see p17.

➡ The airport is connected to central Lisbon by metro (a single costs €1.40). It is the terminus of the red line.

➡ The **AeroBus** (www. yellowbustours.com; one-way €3.50) departs from outside the arrivals hall roughly every 20 minutes from 7am to 11pm. It goes via Marquês de Pombal, Avenida da Liberdade, Restauradores, Rossio and Praça do Comércio

to Cais do Sodré (25 to 35 minutes). The ticket gives free passage on the city bus network for the rest of the day.

➡ A taxi into central Lisbon should cost around €15, plus €1.60 for luggage. Avoid queues by flagging one down at the departures hall.

From Estação Santa Apolónia

➡ Metro services run every few minutes, providing speedy connections to central Lisbon. A single ticket costs €1.40 to anywhere in the city.

➡ Santa Apolónia is on the blue line, one stop from Terreiro do Paço (Praça do Comércio), the heart of downtown Lisbon.

From Gare do Oriente

➡ The ultramodern Gare do Oriente is on the red metro line, which provides quick and frequent connections to central Lisbon.

➡ Baixa-Chiado in central Lisbon is a 20-minute metro ride away. Change for the green line at Alameda.

➡ Bus services linking Gare do Oriente to central Lisbon include the 708 to Martim Moniz (via the airport). Single tickets cost €1.80.

Getting Around

Metro

☑ **Best for...** Short hops and to reach Parque das Nações.

➡ Compact and easy to navigate, the **Lisbon Metro** (www.metrolisboa. pt) has just four lines: red, green, yellow and blue.

➡ The metro runs from 6.30am to 1am.

➡ Buy tickets from the machines at metro stations; a single costs €1.40.

Tickets & Passes

There are two useful cards for catching public transport around the city; both can be purchased from kiosks in the metro stations.

Viva Viagem Costs 50¢, to which you can then add credit in various denominations. Select the 'add credit' option, rather than a single trip (only valid for the metro), which allows the card to be used on the metro, buses, trams and funiculars.

24-hour Carris/metro pass Costs €6 and allows unlimited travel over a 24-hour period on all buses, trams, funiculars and the metro.

➡ Validate your ticket at the station entrance.

➡ Useful signs include 'correspondência' (transfer between lines) and 'saída' (exit to the street).

Tram, Bus & Funicular

☑ **Best for...** Sightseeing as you go from A to B.

➡ **Carris** (www.carris.pt) operates all transport except the metro.

➡ Buses and trams run from about 5am or 6am to 1am; there are some night bus and tram services.

➡ Pick up a transport map from tourist offices or Carris kiosks, which are dotted around the city. The Carris website has timetables and route details.

➡ Individual tickets cost €1.80 on buses, €2.85 on trams; they can be purchased on board. Buy 24-hour Carris passes (€6) from ticket machines or kiosks at metro stations.

➡ A return funicular journey costs €3.60, except the Elevador de Santa Justa, which costs €5.

➡ Always validate your ticket.

Bicycle

☑ **Best for...** Free-wheeling along the riverfront.

➡ Traffic, trams, hills and cobbles make cycling a challenging prospect. There are pleasant rides along a new bike lane beside the Rio Tejo, however.

Taxi

☑ **Best for...** Short hops and journeys involving luggage.

➡ Taxis in Lisbon are plentiful. Try the ranks at Rossio and Praça dos Restauradores, near stations and ferry terminals, or call **Rádio Táxis** (☏ 218 119 000; www.taxislisboa.pt).

➡ The fare on the meter should read €2.50 (daytime flag fall).

➡ You will be charged extra for luggage and 20% more for journeys from 9pm to 6am.

Essential Information

Business Hours

☑ **Top Tip** Many shops close on Sundays and some shut early on Saturdays; small boutiques may also close for lunch (1pm to 3pm). Monday is the day of rest for most museums – check the opening hours we give in specific reviews.

Exceptions to the following opening hours are noted in listings:

Bars	7pm-3am
Cafes	8am-midnight
Clubs	11pm-6am Thu-Sat
Restaurants	lunch noon-3pm, dinner 7-10pm
Shops	9.30am-7pm Mon-Fri, 9.30am-1pm Sat

Discount Cards

The **Lisboa Card** represents excellent value, offering unlimited use of public transport (including trains to Sintra and Cascais), entry to all key museums and attractions, plus up to 50% discount on tours, cruises and other admission charges. It's available at **Ask Me Lisboa** (www.askmelisboa.com) tourist offices, including the one at the airport. The 24-/48-/72-hour versions cost €18.50/31.50/39. Validate the card when you want to start it.

Electricity

230V/50Hz

120V/60Hz

Emergency

Police, Fire & Ambulance (📞112)

Money

☑ **Top Tip** Some small, family-run shops, restaurants and even guesthouses accept cash only. If in doubt, ask before you pay.

➡ The Portuguese currency is the euro (€), divided into 100 cents.

➡ Visa is widely accepted, as is MasterCard; American Express and Diners Club less so, with the exception of top-end hotels and restaurants.

➡ Many automated services, such as ticket machines, require a chip-and-pin credit card.

➡ ATMs (Multibancos) are the easiest way to access your money. You just need your card and PIN. Your home bank will usually charge around 1.5% per transaction.

➡ Service is not usually added to the bill. Tip 5% to 10% for good service in restaurants. Round up to the nearest €1 in cafes and taxis.

Public Holidays

New Year's Day 1 January

Carnival Tuesday February/March; the day before Ash Wednesday

Good Friday March/April

Liberty Day 25 April; celebrating the 1974 revolution

Labour Day 1 May

Corpus Christi May/June; the ninth Thursday after Easter

Portugal Day 10 June; also known as Camões and Communities Day

St Anthony's Day 13 June

Feast of the Assumption 15 August

Republic Day 5 October; commemorating the 1910 declaration of the Portuguese Republic

All Saint's Day 1 November

Independence Day 1 December; commemorating the 1640 restoration of independence from Spain

Feast of the Immaculate Conception 8 December

Christmas Day 25 December

Safe Travel

☑ **Top Tip** Watch out for pickpockets in rush-hour crowds.

➡ Mind your wallet on tram 28 – a major hot spot for pickpockets – and at other tourist hubs such as Rua Augusta and *miradouro* (viewpoint) cafes.

➡ You might be offered hash and sunglasses in Baixa and Bairro Alto; a firm but polite 'no' keeps hawkers at bay.

➡ Main streets are relatively safe to walk along at night, but be wary around metro stations such as Anjos, Martim Moniz and Intendente, where there have been muggings.

➡ Take care in the dark alleys of Alfama and Graça.

Telephone

☑ **Top Tip** Buy a local SIM card to save on roaming charges.

➡ Most payphones require a phonecard, available in denominations of €3, €6 and €9. Buy them at post and telephone offices and newsagents.

➡ There are discount call shops doubling as internet cafes around Largo de São Domingos (B2).

Money-Saving Tips

➡ If you're on a budget, save your sightseeing for Sunday mornings, when entry to the majority of Lisbon's museums is free.

➡ Most sights have concessions (up to 50%) for youths, students and seniors – make sure you bring appropriate ID.

➡ Lisbon's top sights and attractions usually offer free entry for children under 12 (occasionally under 14).

Toilets

☑ **Top Tip** Train, metro and bus stations generally have public conveniences.

➡ Public toilets are few and far between.

➡ Your best bet is to pop into a cafe or bar. If you only want to use the loo, order a *bica* (espresso), one of the cheapest things on the menu.

Tourist Information

Central Offices

Tourist Office (Map p28, D2; ☎ 213 463 314; www.askmelisboa.com; Palácio Foz, Praça dos Restauradores; ◷9am-8pm) Staff dole out maps and information, book accommodation or reserve rental cars.

Lisboa Welcome Centre (Map p46, C5; ☎ 210 312 810; www.visitlisboa.com; Praça do Comércio; ◷9am-8pm) Main branch of Turismo de Lisboa, providing free city maps, brochures, and hotel and tour booking services. Buy the Lisboa Card (p149) here.

Kiosks

Information Kiosk (☎218 450 660; Airport; ◷7am-midnight) In the arrivals hall.

Information Kiosk (Map p82, C3; ☎213 658 435; Largo dos Jerónimos, Belém; ◷10am-1pm & 2-6pm Mon-Sat) Centrally located in Belém.

Information Kiosk (Map p64, G3; ☎218 821 606; Door 47, Santa Apolónia train station; ◷7.30am-10pm Mon-Sat) Situated inside Santa Apolónia train station.

Language

Most sounds in Portuguese are also found in English. The exceptions are the nasal vowels (represented in our pronunciation guides by 'ng' after the vowel), pronounced as if you're trying to make the sound through your nose; and the strongly rolled *r* (represented by 'rr' in our pronunciation guides). Also note that the symbol 'zh' sounds like the 's' in 'pleasure'. Keeping these few points in mind and reading the pronunciation guides as if they were English, you'll be understood just fine. The stressed syllables are indicated with italics.

To enhance your trip with a phrasebook, visit **lonelyplanet.com**.

Basics

Hello.
Olá. o·*laa*

Goodbye.
Adeus. a·de·*oosh*

How are you?
Como está? ko·moo shtaa

Fine, and you?
Bem, e você? beng e vo·se

Please.
Por favor. poor fa·vor

Thank you.
Obrigado. (m) o·bree·gaa·doo
Obrigada. (f) o·bree·gaa·da

Excuse me.
Faz favor. faash fa·vor

Sorry.
Desculpe. desh·kool·pe

Yes./No.
Sim./Não. seeng/nowng

I don't understand.
Não entendo. nowng eng·teng·doo

Do you speak English?
Fala inglês? faa·la eeng·glesh

Eating & Drinking

..., please.
..., por favor. ... poor fa·vor

A coffee	*Um café*	oong ka·fe
A table for two	*Uma mesa para duas pessoas*	oo·ma me·za pa·ra doo·ash pe·so·ash
Two beers	*Dois cervejas*	doysh ser·ve·zhash

I'm a vegetarian.
Eu sou e·oo soh
vegetariano/ ve·zhe·a·ree·a·noo/
vegetariana. (m/f) ve·zhe·a·ree·a·na

Cheers!
Saúde! sa·oo·de

That was delicious!
Isto estava eesh·too shtaa·va
delicioso. de·lee·see·o·zoo

The bill, please.
A conta, por favor. a kong·ta poor fa·vor

Shopping

I'd like to buy ...
Queria ke·ree·a
comprar ... kong·praar ...

I'm just looking.
Estou só a ver. shtoh so a ver

How much is it?
Quanto custa? kwang·too koosh·ta

It's too expensive.
Está muito shtaa *mweeng·*too
caro. kaa·roo

Can you lower the price?
Pode baixar po·de bai·*shaar*
o preço? oo pre·soo

Emergencies

Help!
Socorro! soo·ko·rroo

Call a doctor!
Chame um shaa·me oong
médico! me·dee·koo

Call the police!
Chame a shaa·me a
polícia! poo·lee·sya

I'm sick.
Estou doente. shtoh doo·eng·te

I'm lost.
Estou perdido. (m) shtoh per·dee·doo
Estou perdida. (f) shtoh per·dee·da

Where's the toilet?
Onde é a casa de ong·de e a kaa·za de
banho? ba·nyoo

Time & Numbers

What time is it?
Que horas são? kee o·rash sowng

It's (10) o'clock.
São (dez) horas. sowng (desh) o·rash

Half past (10).
(Dez) e meia. (desh) e may·a

morning	*manhã*	ma·nyang
afternoon	*tarde*	taar·de
evening	*noite*	noy·te
yesterday	*ontem*	ong·teng

today	*hoje*	o·zhe
tomorrow	*amanhã*	aa·ma·nyang

1	*um*	oong
2	*dois*	doysh
3	*três*	tresh
4	*quatro*	kwaa·troo
5	*cinco*	seeng·koo
6	*seis*	saysh
7	*sete*	se·te
8	*oito*	oy·too
9	*nove*	no·ve
10	*dez*	desh

Transport & Directions

Where's ...?
Onde é ...? ong·de e ...

What's the address?
Qual é o kwaal e oo
endereço? eng·de·re·soo

Can you show me (on the map)?
Pode-me po·de·me
mostrar moosh·traar
(no mapa)? (noo maa·pa)

When's the next bus?
Quando é que sai kwang·doo e ke sai
o próximo oo pro·see·moo
autocarro? ow·to·kaa·rroo

I want to go to ...
Queria ir a ... ke·ree·a eer a ...

Does it stop at ...?
Pára em ...? paa·ra eng ...

Please stop here.
Por favor pare poor fa·vor paa·re
aqui. a·kee

Behind the Scenes

Send Us Your Feedback

We love to hear from travellers – your comments help make our books better. We read every word, and we guarantee that your feedback goes straight to the authors. Visit **lonelyplanet.com/contact** to submit your updates and suggestions.

Note: We may edit, reproduce and incorporate your comments in Lonely Planet products such as guidebooks, websites and digital products, so let us know if you don't want your comments reproduced or your name acknowledged. For a copy of our privacy policy visit lonelyplanet.com/privacy.

Our Readers

Many thanks to the travellers who wrote to us with useful advice and anecdotes:

Alessio Fabrizi, Jason Fung, Charlotte Kerr, Jeroen Lemkes, David Powell, Judith van Seeters, Alda Traversi, Wim Vandenbussche, John Woodcock

Kerry's Thanks

I am *muito obrigada* to all of the locals, tourism pros and fellow travellers who made this guide possible. I'd like to say a special thank you to Jorge Moita (you are a star!) and to SIC Portugal journalist Rui Pedro Ruis for his invaluable insight and tips.

Acknowledgments

Cover photograph: Elevador da Bica funicular; Matt Munro/Lonely Planet.

This Book

This third edition of Lonely Planet's *Pocket Lisbon* guidebook was researched and written by Kerry Christiani. The first and second editions were also written and researched by Kerry. This guidebook was produced by the following:

Destination Editor Jo Cooke **Product Editors** Penny Cordner, Kate Kiely **Senior Cartographer** Anthony Phelan **Book Designers** Clara Monitto, Wibowo Rusli **Assisting Editors** Carly Hall, Gabrielle Stefanos **Cover Researcher** Naomi Parker **Thanks to** Wayne Murphy, Karyn Noble, Lorna Parkes, Martine Power, Jacqui Saunders, Lyahna Spencer, Lauren Wellicome, Tony Wheeler

Index

Sights **000**
Map Pages **000**

Our Writer

Kerry Christiani

This is the third edition of the *Pocket Lisbon* guide Kerry has authored and the city never ceases to amaze her, with its easygoing locals, pure Atlantic light, hilltop *miradouros* and vibrant nightlife and arts scenes. For this edition, she clicked into the groove of Alfama's *fado* bars, ate fresh seafood at nearby beaches (in autumn), hung out with designers, and found a raft of new boutiques, bars, restaurants and galleries that are making the Portuguese capital one of Europe's most exciting.

Kerry studied Portuguese translation as part of her MA at the University of Westminster before going on to author numerous guidebooks, including around a dozen Lonely Planet titles. She tweets @kerrychristiani and lists her latest work at www.kerrychristiani.com.

Published by Lonely Planet Publications Pty Ltd
ABN 36 005 607 983
3rd edition – Oct 2015
ISBN 978 1 74321 562 3
© Lonely Planet 2015 Photographs © as indicated 2015
10 9 8 7 6 5 4 3 2 1
Printed in China